LOGAN SEELYE IS A HUSBAND, a father, a brother, a son and a "glass-is-half-full" kind of guy. He lives his life with a purpose and goal to inspire all those he can, and is on a mission to share his story to all those who will listen.

Testimonials about how Logan has impacted his peers.

"You never gave up. I saw the determination you had and you inspired me to continue pursuing my education. I completed my MBA in 2013. I was ready to give up during my AA because work, raising a family and ultimately divorce seemed like too much of a challenge. But I saw your determination and you never gave up, and I see where you are now; you are an amazing human being and I am so grateful to know you."

- Patricia Sierra (junior high/high school friend's mom)

"If you know Logan, at least as long as I have, you know three things: He's extremely intelligent, charismatic, hardworking, and damn funny. I remember sitting in class in seventh, 10th, whatever year, with Logan cracking jokes, talking about the upcoming game or how hungry we were. I always thought, this is one talented motherf---er. He's smart, athletic as hell, and all the ladies love him–he had the golden ticket. When he was injured, I was maybe 50-100 feet away, and all I could think about was, why him? If anyone had a chance at greatness, it was Logan. It wasn't until I was an adult did I understand: it happened to Logan because he truly was destined for greatness, and nothing would stop him. To this day, Logan has the same passion and fire in his eyes as he did 13 years ago when he was making highlight reels every week. The reality is, Logan won. Nobody has a heart like him, a true champion. He continues to inspire, motivate, and move people every day; instead of doing it with his body, he's doing it with a disciplined mind and unwavering heart. He lives this life boldly with the greatest enthusiasms, and he's got an amazing partner in crime (she might be stronger), Jordyn. You're an exceptional human being, and it's an honor to call you my friend. I love you, brother! PTP."

- Mike Savageau (friend, West Point graduate)

"People face different challenges throughout life. Some challenges require exceptional effort to overcome. The mechanism you use daily to normalize your life comes from within Logan. Only you know how to draw from it, where it comes from, and what level it takes you. I hope your book enlightens others about your mechanism. Our best guess it is family– and friend–based. Growing up, your family taught you values such as love, compassion, caring, beliefs, and a sense of fairness. Add the competitive nature sports instilled, plus the great feeling of accomplishment; you were destined to be successful in life. Go Hawks!"

- Mike Riley (Jordyn's uncle on her dad's side)

"I've known Logan Seelye for over 15 years now. We happened to meet right after he had his accident. I didn't know the man he was before, but I can tell you that no matter what he was always a positive, funny and caring man. I've served in the military for going on nine years now, and I've known men to receive lesser injuries and it destroyed them. He is truly an inspiration to me, and he should be to many others. I'm proud to be able to call him my friend."

- Ryan Salvat (friend, United States Military)

"You're amazing, Logan. God is using your story to reach many people who need to know that through incredible adversity they can find incredible power. Love you man!"

- Jeff Thorp (friend, EMT)

"I remember watching you get up and walk at graduation. Even my dad got teary-eyed. I've been sick since after high school, and that's one of the things that kept me going and fighting. 'Logan got the f--- up and walked. You can get up too.'"

- Amanda Allen (friend)

"I didn't really get close to you until your accident. You invited me to be part of your rehab and to watch while you worked out. What an honor to watch. Your tenacity is amazing! Your determination to see it through no matter how long it took and what the cost has me in awe. I love seeing what you have done with your life. You are a fabulous husband, loving father, and an all-around great person. On my birthday I went to the football game and watched you walk out on the field for the first time. It was such an awesome thing to see, and I'll never forget it. To see you was one of the best birthday presents I could have received."

- Janine Fleming (friend, Brandon Fleming's mom)

"You inspired so many people, Logan. We thought we were there for you, but through your journey WE learned to believe above and beyond. Thank you, and we love you!"

- Michelle Easterly (friend, Steven Easterly's mom)

"Just wanted you to know although we were never the closest of friends, I always respected you and always looked up to you.

You are truly an inspiration and your story is one to tell, that's for sure. I still remember that day at camp like it was yesterday and it changed me forever and I realized how life can change in an instant. Although you were faced with a situation most 16-year-olds couldn't handle, you showed us all that everything happens for a reason and you made the most of your injury and didn't let it slow you down at all. Seeing you cut the ribbon at Art Crate was also a tremendous achievement and I'm glad I could see you take those steps. I just want you to know you're a great person and an inspiration to many. God bless you, Logan."

- Jeff Webb (friend)

"When life gets tough, the tough get going. This outlook on life is something I was taught as a child and am reminded of when I think about you. From the awesome times we had playing ball, to helping each other through schoolwork, I could tell I had met a genuinely good person with a drive to not only succeed but to help those around him succeed. The life-changing effects your accident caused you to go through would have weakened and even broken most. However, your ability to focus on the 10 & 90 mentality and stay positive in the face of adversity have put you in the position of a modern-day inspirational role model. I hope this book can help you continue to positively change lives. Time may pass and life moves on, but a football brotherhood lives forever. "

- Jacob Skordal (friend, former high school teammate)

10 AND 90

The Tackle That Changed Everything

Kitty,

Thanks for all the support!

#10 and 90

Logan Seelye

Book and cover design by Logan Seelye
Book cover photography by John Froschauer
Initial editing by Natalia Ross
Proofread by Sandy Deneau Dunham

For more information, and to see pictures: www.10and90.com

ISBN: 978-0-692-57453-9

First Edition

10 9 8 7 6 5 4 3 2 1

CONTENTS

To my amazingly wonderful wife, Jordyn, and to our beautiful daughter, Skylar. Without them, I truly don't know where I'd be. I have gone through a lot in my life so far, and I know the road is still steep and treacherous, but with them by my side I know I can accomplish anything. I cherish you both so much, and I love you to the moon and back.

The longer I live, the more I realize the impact of attitude on life. Attitude, to me, is more important than facts. It is more important than the past, than education, than money, than circumstances, than failures, than successes, than what other people think or say or do. It is more important than appearance, giftedness, or skill. It will make or break a company ... a church ... a home. The remarkable thing is we have a choice every day regarding the attitude we will embrace for that day. We cannot change the inevitable. The only thing we can do is play on the one string we have, and that is our attitude ... I am convinced that life is 10% what happens to me, and 90% how I react to it. And so it is with you ... we are in charge of our Attitudes.

- CHARLES SWINDOLL, "Attitude"

INTRODUCTION

ON JULY 2, 2003, I was a 16-year-old kid with a great life: a beautiful girlfriend whom I began dating in junior high school; friends who would do anything for me and vice versa; a father who cooked me steak and eggs every morning for breakfast and an older brother who had been rooting me on since the day I was old enough to pick up a ball; a football coach and teammates who wholeheartedly believed in me and my potential for unlimited success.

I knew exactly where my life was heading, and I had no doubt that football was going to be forever etched at the front and center of the picture.

Then something happened. The door to the life I believed I was meant to live got slammed shut in my face. I got hurt, and it wasn't the kind of injury you could get up, dust yourself off, and walk away from. Instead of aggressively charging forward to make the next big play on the football field, I was gently rolling through the corridors of a rehab hospital in a wheelchair. I was told that I would never walk again, that I would never even have any feeling or movement from my chest down. That vibrant, colorful picture of what my life was going to be was stripped down from the wall and replaced by … something very different.

Potentially, that picture could have been filled with dark clouds and gloomy skies, featuring an angry, bitter kid who constantly whined about what happened to him, obsessed over what might have been, and moped around in a life with no purpose or meaning, no real joy or vitality. But I knew from the day I awoke from spinal cord surgery that this was a picture that I would *never* step into. I would never ask, "Why me?" Instead I would ask other questions: What can I do to regain strength in my body and progress toward walking on my own someday? What new workout can I take on at the gym? How can I be the best husband to that girlfriend from junior high school, and the best father of a radiant and lively 3-year-old girl? What can I do to continue to learn and improve my performance at work? Where might there be another sports team, a group of school kids, or a business or organization that could benefit from my talk about what happened to me and what I've made of it?

I'm still living a great life. It's just a different picture. Every morning, I feel thankful and blessed to wake up and live another day in the picture I'm in. Yes, I've had to endure my share of pain and challenges. Who doesn't? The way I look at it, you can either choose to be negative and complain, or you can choose to maintain a positive outlook and face each and every challenge, setback, or struggle head-on, determined to persevere no matter what.

What happened to me is a part of my life—but really, it's only a small part. I've adopted a spirit and philosophy called the "10 and 90" approach to life. It is a mindset that stems from this quote: "Life is 10 percent what happens to you and 90 percent how you react to it." This idea was introduced by Charles Swindoll, an insightful theologian and author. To me, it means that my life is not defined by the accident I suffered on a football field more than 12 years ago. It is defined by everything I do, and everything I am, here and now. No matter what happened to me, I can choose how I respond to it and what path I will follow. I embrace the life I'm living, and I believe that God has chosen me to live it because he knows I am strong enough to take it on.

I'd like to tell you my story. In the pages ahead, you will hear about my life before my football injury and how that experience impacted me and all those who care about me. You'll hear about the incredible support, encouragement, and hands-on assistance that I have consistently received from so many people who know me well, and others who learned about my situation and felt moved to find some way to respond. I'll take you inside many of my triumphant moments, and I'll be as honest as I can about what's been hard for me and share those times when I didn't have all the answers. I will especially try to convey the love and gratitude that fill my days.

My hope is that my story, and the message of living the 10 and 90 life, will speak to you in some way. Maybe you, or someone you love, have had something bad happen—some setback, loss, or accident that transformed the picture of your or their life. Perhaps something you read in my book will touch you, encourage you, inspire you to keep going, keep battling, keep grasping for the life you *can* live and embrace. And even if you have not had the experience of suffering a major blow, my wish is that you take away something from my book that will somehow, someway elevate how you look at life around you, and remind you of the full potential of the human spirit.

CHAPTER ONE

The Hit

MY DREAM WAS COMING MORE sharply into focus. I could feel it, sense it, almost taste it. Every day, with every big play, I could more clearly see the trail that would lead to playing major college football. Then, if I kept putting in the hard work and dedication, maybe someday that path would wind its way to the NFL. Sure, that's the same dream held by millions of high school football players from Washington State to Washington, D.C., but it was very real to me. I had an inner feeling, a belief in myself that I was going to do something big—and no one or nothing was going to stop me!

Positive signs were busting out all over the field at Central Washington University during that football camp in the summer of 2003. I was revving up for my junior year at

Spanaway Lake High School, with an early recruitment letter from Boise State University already tucked away in my bedroom back home. At camp, opposing coaches and players were paying attention to our team's tough defense and the hard-hitting safety—Number 22, Logan Seelye—who kept making big plays. My coach, John Robak, told the other coaches when camp started that he had a junior who was going to be "something special," and now that player was really opening their eyes.

"Logan was all around the ball, making tackles for loss, and he could really bring it," Coach Ro recalls. "I once coached Lawyer Milloy (a retired NFL safety) in high school, and Logan had that same ability—when he tackled you, he didn't just hit you and stop, he ran right *through* you."

The camp lasted five days and four nights, with most of the early part devoted to team and individual drills. As camp heated up, so did the action. Each school faced off against other teams from all over the state in short, intense scrimmages. I remember one play early in camp:

The other team's wide receiver was lined up on the outside and then went in motion toward the other side. I noticed that he was moving pretty quickly. I had been getting better and better at diagnosing plays, and I just had a feeling the play was going to be a sweep to that receiver. So I positioned myself right behind our outside linebacker, giving him a little hand signal to tip him off about the play I knew was coming. The quarterback took the snap and, sure enough, just as I ran past him, he handed the ball off to that receiver. In a flash I was in that guy's face, blowing up the play and making a huge tackle for a loss.

Some days of camp wrapped up with "the challenge." After you challenged another team and that team accepted, each side got five plays to score from the 25-yard line, sort of like overtime in college football. One day we were challenged by White River High, and man, did they choose the wrong team to take on! From the beginning of camp we had been demonstrating that we were fast, precise, on-point with our execution, and totally ready to go.

On our team's first play, Maurice Jones, our top running back, ran the ball in for a touchdown. With our whole team fired up, we switched sides to go on defense. On the first play, my gut said: "It's a run up the middle." That's exactly what they called. I came crashing down from my safety spot and smashed into the running back, jarring him backwards. As I immediately popped up, waving my arms, the enthusiasm shot through our whole team. White River tried another play, this time a run to the left, and we tackled the ball-carrier for a loss again. When we stuffed the next play too, the White River coach said, "That's it; we're done." He did not even want to complete the challenge. As I sprinted to our sideline, I yelled to Bryan Davis, one of our assistant coaches, "Let's play more! Let's go!" He slapped my helmet as my teammates whooped and hollered.

Unfortunately, there wasn't going to be one more play … at least that time. We carried our enthusiasm back to the dorms, and as we tore off our uniforms and charged into the showers, we felt like we just couldn't wait for the next day of camp. It was the final day, and it was going to be all scrimmages, no drills.

I can't say we got much sleep that night, with six players crammed into each three-bedroom dorm suite. I was sharing a suite with Steven Easterly and Brandon Fleming, my main training buddies during the killer workouts we gutted through back at school that spring, when I beefed up from about 155 to 185 pounds while increasing my strength and speed. Maurice Jones was in our dorm suite too, along with Anthony Rios and Steven Parley. We were loaded up with candy and snacks, along with a bunch of movies and, of course, an Xbox to play all our favorite video games. The dorms were hot, sweaty, loud … and we were having a blast!

For the final day of camp, each team scrimmaged against three opponents. The scrimmages consisted of each team running 10 plays on offense and 10 plays on defense. We cruised through our first matchup, running over everything in our path and winning easily. As one of our team captains, I was thinking to myself, "Man, we've got a good thing going here. We're playing with so much poise and grit. I bet we're going to have a great season; maybe even play for the state 4A championship."

The opposing team for the next scrimmage was Redmond High from east of Seattle, a good bit up the road from Spanaway, which is just south of Tacoma. Redmond was a solid team, but we were playing with complete confidence, especially on defense. Our offense also was in sync, as once again we scored easily on our first series of plays. Then it was time for our defense to show its stuff. Ten plays later, after denying Redmond any opportunity to score, we were trudging triumphantly toward the sidelines, eager for our offense to take over to run the next 10 plays.

Suddenly, Tom Brokaw, our defensive coordinator who just happens to have the same name as the famous TV newsman, called out, "Let's run one more play!" After the Redmond coach nodded in agreement, our defense hustled back onto the field and eagerly huddled up.

"One more play! Let's go!" one of my teammates barked.

Here's what happened next:

We are in a "cover 2" defense, which means Willie Davis, our other safety, and I are each covering half the field in support of our linebackers and cornerbacks. The ball snaps. I make my read. I notice that the slot receiver has started running straight ahead, but his body language tells me he's going to run a post route, where the receiver runs out seven to 10 yards and then cuts toward the middle of the field. I glance at the quarterback. "Yep, he's definitely throwing it to this receiver on the post play," I say to myself.

I dig my feet in and sprint toward the area where I think the ball will arrive. I'm going to time my hit to come right when the ball arrives and knock it loose, making one more big play for our defense. I say to myself, "Man, this is going to be a kill shot!"

As I close in, the receiver jumps to try to catch the pass. I'm relying on instinct and not thinking about this, but somewhere in the back of my mind are the echoing voices of my coaches and teammates who have been telling me for months, "Keep your head up when you tackle, Logan!" I'm known for tackling with my head down because at 5-10 I'm smaller than most of the other players I go up against, so when I tackle, I charge with my head lowered and go for their thighs. But tackling with your head down puts you at greater risk of a neck injury—you don't want to "see grass" when you hit the guy. So this time, without being aware of trying to do it differently, I keep my head up as I burst into that receiver.

Wham!

I just destroy the guy. The ball jars loose, and Willie intercepts it and starts running it back for a touchdown, with our whole defense running with him and the rest of our team jumping up and down and screaming on the sidelines, celebrating my perfect tackle.

Except the receiver is still down on the ground. So am I. And I am not moving.

That was The Hit that forever changed my life, the tackle that would change everything and shatter my dream of building a football reputation as a tough, smart, hard-hitting safety during two more seasons at Spanaway Lake High, then earning a scholarship to play for Boise State, or maybe the University of Washington, and then four or five years later catching on with an NFL team, preferably my hometown Seattle Seahawks. Now that dream was gone—poof—just like that!

Coach Ro told me later that the way the Redmond High receiver jumped up and twisted, my helmet smacked right into his chest, kind of under his armpit, causing my head to snap violently to the left. It was a fluke play, really. But that's football. It's a physical sport, and you can get hurt at any time, in any way. There I was, finally tackling the way you're supposed to tackle, keeping my head up and always seeing what's in front of me, and I break my neck ....

Still, I have to be honest about The Hit. I really did want to destroy that receiver. That's just how I approached the game, and how I was going to continue to carry myself. That was the mindset that would take me as far as I would have been able to go in the game.

Down there on the grass of the football field at Central Washington University, in the hot sun of this July 2, 2003, afternoon, I was not thinking about any of that. All I knew was that everyone and everything had gone silent and I was surrounded by guys from the university's training staff, and my own coaches, and then pretty soon the emergency personnel who had rushed to the scene. And still I was not moving. I knew something must be wrong. I had suffered a few stingers in the past where my vision kind of went green and I felt woozy, to the point where I should have taken myself off the field but just kept on going anyway. This was nothing like that. I was lying on the ground in a fetal position. My helmet was facing left, with my right side down on the grass. I could see my left hand out in front of me, and I tried over and over again to move it. Nothing.

Fortunately, I was breathing on my own and able to talk to the medical staff, although my voice was soft and feeble. I remember my defensive backs coach, Bryan Corpus, kneeling down and looking at me through my facemask.

"You OK?" he asked.

"I don't know," I mumbled. "I can't move. I can't feel anything."

And then Coach Ro was there. Here's how he remembers it:

"I can still close my eyes and see the picture in my mind after I sprinted onto the field. Logan's lying on the ground with his hands across himself, and he's telling me, 'Coach, I can't feel my body; my body's on fire.' My heart just went ka-boom. He didn't move an inch."

The next 30 minutes, or however long I stayed on that turf, was the strangest and scariest half-hour of my life. It was also the period of time that the training staff most likely saved my life, while also helping to leave a door slightly open to a journey that I hope someday will lead to walking on my own. As I would learn much, much later, when you break your neck it's not the breaking of the vertebrae that causes the damage and leaves you with paralysis; it's the swelling of the spine. I'm no medical expert, but from what I understand the spinal cord is a complex bundling of nerves with each section controlling a different function or muscle of your body. The higher up your neck the damage is, and the closer to your brain, the more it affects your body and limbs. In the initial moments after the injury occurs, spinal cord damage can be greatly increased by any movement. So it's absolutely critical that no one moves the head or neck area *at all*, unless the person is specifically trained in how to do so safely. If the head moves, it can cause much worse damage to the spinal cord, resulting in a far lesser chance of ever regaining movement, feeling, or strength throughout the body. And there was at least one member of the attending staff who did at first suggest that they remove my helmet.

"No, DO NOT remove the helmet," one of the Central Washington trainers said firmly. "We need to leave that on and get him stabilized first. His helmet can be removed later."

Fortunately, this plea was echoed by others in the circle around me, including Coach Ro. They recognized that getting a helmet off a player isn't easy. They would have had to move my head back and forth, which definitely could have worsened my neck damage. After they came to agreement not to risk such movement, they set out to roll me over onto my back and get me on the stretcher. In my limited awareness of my body, I believed I was in the total fetal position, my legs bent up to my chest. In reality, I was lying mostly straight, with just a slight bend in my knees.

All this time, I still had the sensation of my body being on fire. You know that feeling when your foot falls asleep and then it starts waking up, with that tingly, burning? For me, that tingling and burning sensation, in high intensity, extended over my entire body.

They managed to get me on the stretcher, very slowly. I had the sense of moving but not feeling as if I was moving. All I knew was that I was on the stretcher and it was rolling toward the ambulance. I was also aware that my teammates, as well as the Redmond High players and coaches, along with players and coaches assembling from all the other teams that had stopped their own scrimmages at other locations around camp, were all watching me. And they were worried about how bad it was. That's when I had the idea that I would give the "thumbs up" sign.

It's a strange coincidence that the football player generally given credit for starting the "thumbs up" tradition also happened to come from my area of Washington. Mike Utley played for Kennedy High School in Burien, between Seattle and Tacoma, and went on to Washington State University before starting an NFL career as an offensive lineman with the Detroit Lions. During a Nov. 17, 1991, home game against the Los Angeles Rams, Mike suffered a spinal cord injury while pass-blocking and, although he would later discover that he was mostly paralyzed from the chest down, he was able to flash a "thumbs up" sign as he was carried from the field on a stretcher to let everyone know he was going to be all right. From then on, almost every football player who gets badly hurt and has to be carried off the field gives the same sign ... or tries to.

I can't tell you how bad I wanted to give that thumbs-up sign. I tried with all my might, and then I closed my eyes and tried again. I just couldn't move my arm or my hand. Instead of showing to myself and my teammates and onlookers that I was OK, I lay motionless on the stretcher as the ambulance prepared to rush me to the nearest hospital.

Soon after I arrived at Kittitas Valley Community Hospital in Ellensburg, the town where Central Washington University is located, I was given a shot of steroids in my neck to try to slow the swelling. Though major damage had already been done, this intervention was another important contributor to any hopes of gaining a degree of recovery. I know that Ro was all over the hospital staff urging them to use the steroid treatment because he was aware that the steroid drip was, at that time, the most effective way to reduce swelling of the spinal cord. Not many years later, hypothermia treatment prompted by a cold saline solution became a more advanced treatment, helping Buffalo Bills' tight end Kevin Everett walk only months after going down with a spinal cord injury during an NFL game in 2007.

I was still conscious, aware of everything going on around me at the hospital. The nurse, doctors, and other hospital staff very carefully worked to remove my helmet, unscrew my facemask, and cut off most of my Spanaway Lake High uniform. I still had my pads on, as well as a "butt pad," which covers your tailbone. The staff didn't even know that was there, and I wasn't about to tell them. I wound up with an extremely bad sore from lying on it so long.

At some point I heard a nurse say, "Logan, we have to insert a catheter into your urethra." After a brief pause to absorb what this meant, I said, "OK, but can you tell me when you're going to do it so I can brace for the pain?" She replied, "I already did it." That was another reminder that I couldn't feel anything, couldn't move anything.

The Kittitas staff treated me well, but with the limited facilities of a small, local hospital they knew I would need to be moved to a larger medical facility that could provide more complete and effective spinal cord injury treatment. They assumed that my next stop would be Yakima Valley Memorial Hospital, about 40 miles from Ellensburg. Coach Ro had other ideas.

"No, he's going to Harborview! We've got to get him to Harborview," he said.

Harborview Medical Center in Seattle has a fantastic reputation for handling trauma patients, including spinal cord victims. And with all my family hours away from the scene of my accident, Ro understood that he was the one person who could be relied on to look out for me. To this day, I am grateful for just how seriously he took ownership of this role. That was only the beginning of what Ro would do for me in the aftermath of the injury that changed my life.

So the decision was made to arrange for a helicopter to airlift me the 100-plus miles to Seattle. Meanwhile, Ro understood something else: He had to call my father. As he waited for my dad to answer the phone, he struggled to figure out the right words.

"Well, Logan tackled somebody and … well, right now he doesn't have much sensation below his neck. But we're hoping that he's going to be OK," he explained.

My dad dropped to his knees. He asked to speak to one of the doctors, who probably couldn't tell him much more. Not long after my dad agreed with the plan to send me to Harborview, I was in the air.

The only way I know how to describe my memory of the helicopter ride to Harborview and my first hours there is to compare it to the device they often use in TV shows or movies: You close your eyes and then, when you open them again, you're in a totally different place. In my heavily drugged state, that's how it was for me:

Eyes open: I can see the blue sky above while being transported from the hospital to the copter. Eyes close.

Eyes open: I am smack in the middle of a new hospital. Eyes close.

Eyes open: I see my parents. I have no idea what is said, aware only of my determination not to allow them to see any fear in my eyes. I am told later that the first words I spoke to my dad were, "I got to ride in a helicopter!" Eyes close.

Eyes open. I am flat on my back in a dark room. A doctor is leaning over me and I'm aware that I've got one of those scary-looking halos around my neck. I realize that they had to shave both sides of my head so a screw could go in each side to hold my neck halo in place. This doctor is moving the halo back and forth ever so slightly, millimeter by millimeter, trying to adjust the vertebrae. Somehow I understand that I am being prepped for surgery. As he moves the halo, he is taking X-rays and checking them. This goes on for half an hour, an hour, maybe two. It seems like forever. I can't really feel anything in most of my body, but with the little bit of feeling that I do have, this process seems like the most painful thing I have ever experienced. And then my eyes close once again.

While all this was playing out in my eyes close/eyes open movie scenes, there was much frantic action happening in many other locations. Family, friends, and teammates had either witnessed the accident at camp, or they had heard the news and rushed to be with me. Here are some of their stories:

Steven, teammate and friend: *After Logan's hit caused the interception and we ran it back for a touchdown, I was starting to take the field for offense. Then time just stopped. When I saw Logan not moving like that, I didn't blink for what seemed like minutes. All the games going on at camp stopped. The rest of the scrimmages were cancelled, and the coaches told us we should go to the dorms, get our stuff, and get on the bus to go home. The feeling on that bus was much worse than losing a championship game. We had lost Logan, one of our leaders. After the great camp we had, all the oomph had been taken out of us. We were quiet, full of questions that could not be answered. And still I kept thinking: It was the most perfect tackle.*

Brandon, teammate and friend: *Before it happened I was on the sidelines, just thinking to myself, "Oh my God, we're gonna be killers this year." When I saw that receiver go out on the post pattern and I knew that Logan had read it, I said, "He's gonna kill this guy." And he finally tackled the way we had been telling him to, with his facemask up. Then, when Logan was not moving, I was down on my knee praying for him. He was down a long time and it looked bad, real bad. You never want to see anything like that, whether it's someone on your team or the other team. It's strange but around the same time, in another scrimmage, a player suffered a double compound fracture. So there were actually two ambulances there at camp. It's one of those moments when you realize your own mortality. This is football; things happen. You just never think it's going to happen to someone like*

Logan. *He's a great kid, has a ton of integrity, made starter as a sophomore, and was voted team captain the next spring. Yeah, your time in football is finite.*

Coach Robak: *I wanted to ride in the helicopter with Logan, but they wouldn't let me. I told our coaches to just pack up the dorm and bring the team back home. I jumped in the truck of one of my assistants, Rob Hill, and we hit the road for Harborview. I think the trip from Ellensburg to Seattle usually takes about three hours. We did it in two. The whole time we were just praying, telling each other that when we got to Harborview everything was going to be OK. We had lost a former player to a fatal accident away from the football field, and we had our share of fractures and things like that, but we had never had a serious, debilitating injury to a player.*

At Harborview, we had to wait and wait. A bunch of our players had driven up from Spanaway after going home from camp on the bus. We took over a whole waiting room. It must have been at least five or six hours after being with Logan in that hospital back in Ellensburg that I was finally able to see him again. When I walked in his room and saw him with that halo on, I was struck by the look on his face. Not just his expression, but his whole demeanor told me that he was more worried about us than he was about himself. It was like he was saying, "Hey, don't cry. I'll be OK." It was a pretty emotional time.

My brother Adam: *I was working at my job at Canyon Auto Supplies that day when I got the call from one of the Spanaway football coaches. I must have looked pretty out of it because I was just standing there in front of the customers when my boss said, "Adam, what's up? What happened?" I said, "My brother broke his neck. I've got to go." When I first saw him at Harborview, nothing looked different to me. He was still Logan. Then I saw him later with that halo on his neck and I never cried so hard. When we were growing up, all my friends would always say, "Hey, where's your kid brother?" They knew Logan always wanted to be with me. I'm two years older than him, and in some ways he was like my brother and my son at the same time. Now, with his injury, it felt like both of those roles were taken away.*

My dad: *After I got off the phone with Ro and the doctor in Ellensburg, and the decision was made to take Logan to Harborview, I picked up my wife, Sally, and we headed right for Seattle. By this time it was late afternoon, and as everyone who lives around here knows, the traffic is always brutal around Seattle that time of day. But as were driving, the traffic was amazingly light. It felt like Moses parting the Red Sea.*

When we got to Harborview, and we had to wait and wait, his teammates began showing up. I managed a faint smile as Tyler Wells, a big guy, announced, "We bought donuts, but I ate half of them." Then I spotted Ro, and even though we didn't know each other that well back then, we both just lost it: two grown men crying their eyes out. Then I ran into Tom Brokaw, the defensive coordinator, and he was saying maybe it was his fault because he asked for that "one more play." I told him, "No, no, no, don't even think that for a second. Things just happen in life. You can't control it." Today I look at Logan's injury as what you see portrayed in that TV program "In an Instant." Something happens that just changes everything, and so quickly.

Pastor Jim from our church arrived to counsel us. "You can hate God right now," he said, "but understand that there's a plan here." I struggled to take comfort in that thought. Then the doctors came out and informed us that we had two options: Option A, just do nothing and hope things will somehow heal during what would be a very long waiting game; or Option B, do surgery to stabilize his neck. It was very clear that surgery was the way to go.

IT SEEMED AS IF EVERYONE who was special to me was converging on that waiting room at Harborview, but the person who was the most important to me as a 16-year-old boy took the longest to get there. That's because Jordyn, my girlfriend, heard the news in Sacramento, California, where she had recently arrived for a volleyball tournament and a planned follow-up adventure with her mom, Susie, and her sister Kimiko. Jordyn and I had already been dating for more than two years by then. This was not some brief junior high school crush. She was, and still is, my rock. Our connection was so strong that something happened the night before I left for camp at Central Washington that I still can't explain.

"I'm scared," Jordyn told me. We were at my house, the night before the morning I was to leave for camp. Jordyn was going to head to Sacramento a few days later. "I don't know why, but I just feel like something is going to happen to me … or to you."

I tried to listen patiently, but it wasn't like Jordyn to be scared about much of anything. I couldn't see any reason to be worried. When you're 16 years old and a dedicated athlete, you assume you're invincible.

"Everything will be fine," I said. "I'll see you in a week or so."

I'll let Jordyn tell the rest of her story:

The night before Logan's accident, while I was in Sacramento, something else strange happened. I had a burning pain in my neck, and I couldn't think of anything that could have caused it. Did I somehow know what was going to happen to Logan, that he would hurt his neck? I don't have the answer to that question. I just know I didn't sleep much in the hotel, and when I got up late the next morning I asked Mom to go to lunch with me. I don't know why I did that. Usually, before a volleyball event I would want to be with my teammates and just focus on the first game coming up. So I was in the car with Mom when her cell phone rang. When I picked it up, it was Sally.

"Oh, Jordyn, it's you ... how are you doing?" she asked. She was trying to make small talk, but something didn't sound right.

"Can I talk to your Mom?" Sally asked.

Seconds after I handed Mom the phone, she turned pale—total white face.

"Mom! What?" I shouted. She hung up the phone.

"It's OK, Jordyn, it's OK," she said. "Logan got injured and he's ... he's alive."

"What ... alive? What does that mean, Mom?"

She explained what she knew, which wasn't much, and we drove home, 13 hours straight. The truckers were honking at us for driving too fast. I kept banging my head against the front windshield, yelling and crying. I had never behaved like that. The whole time it just felt like I was in someone else's life. When Logan's step-mom called us about midnight and told us they were all going to Harborview very early in the morning, we drove to Logan's house so we could all ride up to Seattle together. That night, I slept in Logan's bed...

When Jordyn finally got to see me at Harborview, I believe I was just about to go in for surgery. I remember clearly the first words I spoke to her:

"Do you still love me?"

I don't know why I asked that; I guess because I was motionless and vulnerable-looking, the opposite of the invincible football player she knew.

"Yes," she said, without hesitation, "and I always will."

In that moment, I knew that no matter what happened in the days, weeks, and months to come, somehow or other everything really was going to be all right.

CHAPTER TWO

The Prognosis

IT WAS NOT LONG AFTER I had recovered from surgery, and one of the doctors was in my room with my dad. I could tell that this doctor was about to tell me something important.

"You broke your neck, and this is what you should expect now," he explained. "You are not going to have any feelings from your nipples down, possibly ever. You're a quadriplegic. You'll be in a wheelchair …"

Before he could say much more, my dad moved in to shield him from me and gently but firmly escorted him toward the corridor. "You need to leave this room now," he said. I don't know what words were exchanged between the doctor and my dad outside my room, but when the doctor came back in he just looked at me a minute. Then he spoke again.

"We have to give you the bad news … but prove us wrong," he said finally, and then turned to leave.

I don't think I responded, but if I had, the words probably would have sounded something like, "OK; I'll do that. Challenge accepted."

As the months and years went on, I would often think back to that original prognosis, and it would give me fuel to keep on pushing in my recovery, to increase my workouts at the gym, to find new ways to move more and more on my own, to keep my spirits up in facing challenge after challenge in daily life as a person with a spinal cord injury. I carried the positive mindset familiar to most dedicated athletes: You tell me I *can't* do something, and I'm going to show you I *can* do it.

But you know what? In those first couple of days in my hospital room at Harborview Medical Center after hearing that bleak outlook about my future, I wasn't thinking, "Oh, I'll show *him*. I'm going to walk someday." My jumbled thoughts, no doubt shaped by the trauma of what happened and the pain medication they were giving me, would have come out more like this: "This guy's crazy. Somebody's just got to show me what to do to get better here so I can get back to my life the way it was as soon as possible."

I was naïve, unable to accept the reality of what had happened and the hardships that lay ahead. In Adam

Taliaferro's book *Miracle in the Making*, he said that as he lay in his hospital room right after he suffered a spinal cord injury making a tackle for Penn State against Ohio State in 2000, he just kept saying to himself, "I can't be paralyzed. I just can't be paralyzed." I didn't even understand what it meant to be paralyzed, to not be able to move or feel much of my body. It just didn't even register. Before this accident happened, I had never had a serious injury: no broken bones, not even a real sprain. The closest thing to an injury I had suffered was a slight groin pull while running track for Cedarcrest Junior High in Spanaway in eighth grade.

Yes, I did have that concussion in ninth grade playing for the Cedarcrest Chargers football team. In those days, junior high in our school system extended through ninth grade, with high school not beginning until 10th grade. We were playing our big rival, Bethel Junior High, which had beaten us the previous two seasons. We were behind 6-0 for much of the game, but we scored with six minutes left to tie it and, with no reliable kicker, we went for the two-point conversion. After we made it, we held on to win 8-6. I can report these details now, but as the dramatic moments of that game unfolded, I actually had no idea what was going on. I don't even remember getting hit during the game, but as it ended, and players on our team were down on the ground crying, I turned to my coach and said, "What happened?

Did we win?" He told me I must have had my bell rung—a concussion. He explained that when I went home I would feel really tired but I should try not to fall asleep because sleeping is bad for a concussion. Everyone was still well behind the curve of safely and appropriately dealing with concussions back then. At Jordyn's house that evening, she kept telling me over and over, "You can't fall asleep! Stay awake!" But the next day I was fine. It must have been a minor concussion. So with this injury at camp, I just didn't understand the seriousness of what had happened.

The surgery itself was mostly a blur. As it was explained to me later, my C6 vertebra was fractured and my C5 vertebra was dislocated. So, in a nutshell, the neurosurgeon and his staff took out the sixth vertebra and replaced it with a titanium vertebra, which they fused with the fifth vertebra. You might think that they would go in from the back of my neck to do their work, but they actually did it from the front. They cut open my neck right around where my esophagus is located. Apparently they just moved my esophagus out of the way, which made it easier to do what was needed. It sounded backwards to me when I heard about it, but whatever they did must have worked because the surgery was deemed a success. My spine had been stabilized.

I didn't concern myself with details of the surgery in that first day or two, and I wasn't focused on the extreme difficulties and challenges ahead. I was just innocently telling my family and friends from the team, "It's fine, I'll be perfectly fine." I didn't just say that so they wouldn't worry about me. I actually *believed* it.

Some people might say it's foolish or impractical to be thinking so far from reality at such a time, but I would disagree. Kevin Everett was thinking the same way after the spinal cord injury he suffered while making a tackle on a kickoff for the Buffalo Bills against the Denver Broncos during the 2007 NFL season. In his book, *Standing Tall,* Kevin reveals that he kept telling himself that he just had a "minor" injury, nothing serious. Looking back, he credited those early self-assurances for motivating him for the battle ahead. If he had allowed himself to think about just how bad he was hurt, it would have been tougher for him to get up off the deck and start doing what he needed to do. It worked that way for me, too. I was naïve but in a positive way—I was gearing up inside for the long, difficult road ahead.

So there I was telling Jordyn, "Don't worry, babe; I'll be fine. I'll be ready to go back to school in a couple of months, and before you know it I'll be back in training for football, then I'll be getting out on the field to start playing again."

There was another reason, as I look at it now, why my thoughts may have been straying so far from reality in the immediate aftermath of the injury and surgery. I just didn't want to let go of that dream: to finish my high school football career with a growing reputation, to play big-time college ball, to surprise everyone by making an NFL roster. In my one and only season of high school football, I was just having too good a time to imagine the possibility of not getting right back in the flow of the team, to be with the guys in the training room, in the locker room, on the field, in the huddle.

I remember my very first face-to-face meeting with Coach Ro. He would always visit the junior high schools that feed into Spanaway Lake High to scout prospective players. The day he came to Cedarcrest Junior High during my ninth grade, I have to admit I was scared of him. As I looked up from eating my lunch in the cafeteria, I could see that he was built really well, big and muscly, and that his head was shaved. He was one of those football coaches who, when you first see him, you say to yourself, "That guy's a bada--." But I mustered up the courage to walk right up to him and say, "Hey Coach, I'm Logan." He just looked at me, handed me a bunch of papers to read, and said, "Hi Logan. I'm Coach Robak and I look forward to coaching you at Spanaway. I've heard a lot about you and can't wait to see what you can do." Whoa, not bad considering I thought he was going to yell at me! And that was just the beginning of discovering that this tough looking coach would turn out to be one of the nicest guys I have ever known.

Coach Ro already had a solid reputation as a coach when he came to Spanaway Lake High in '95. As an assistant coach at Lincoln High, he had coached not only Lawyer Milloy but also future NFL quarterback Jon Kitna. Lawyer played college ball in Seattle for the University of Washington before his pro career with the New England Patriots and later our own Seahawks. Kitna played at Central Washington University, where I was injured, and then had a great career as a quarterback for several NFL teams, including the Dallas Cowboys. Ro told me that when Lawyer Milloy was a freshman, the Lincoln head coach had a rule that freshmen could not play on varsity. After watching Milloy run one play, however, he said, "Freshmen can play varsity." Ro was born and raised outside of Boston, and we would kid him unmercifully about being a New England Patriots' fan. He just gave it right back to us. He was a players' coach. It was obvious he loved being around us, and we felt the same way.

The Spanaway Lake Sentinels didn't win much before Ro came aboard, but by 1999 they made the playoffs, and the next season they won the SPSL (South Puget Sound League) championship and reached the state 4A quarterfinals. I didn't make varsity as a sophomore at the start of the 2002 season, but while playing on the junior varsity team I got the call early to fill an opening created when one of the varsity running backs got injured. I took full advantage of that opening and never gave up my place, both as a running back and a safety. I had to earn the respect of the older kids on the team, but I had already begun to do that even before the season. One day during preseason practice, they had needed a fullback for a drill where the defenders were supposed to practice hitting a ball-carrier. As a tailback, fullback wasn't my position, but I was glad to fill in. The seniors just demolished me, but after each hit I bounced right back up, ready for more. One of those seniors was my own brother, Adam. He had never held anything back going up against me when we were kids, and he sure didn't let up on me on our high school team.

We didn't have a great year, finishing 5-5, but I remember many highlights of that Spanaway Lake High '02 season:

• We were behind Curtis High by two touchdowns when Brandon's jarring tackle caused a fumble, which I recovered and returned 53 yards for a touchdown. At one point on the return, I tripped and almost fell, but my knee did not go down. "Yeah, that was Little Gumby Sophomore taking it all the way," recalls Brandon, remembering that I weighed about 155 pounds then.

• On Homecoming Night against Emerald Ridge, in a game that we won easily, I had only three carries but accumulated 75 yards rushing and scored two touchdowns. On the first one, a "31 gut" call, I ran 50 yards for a score. The next one was for 20-something yards, and the third one was a short TD run. I also started at safety, making about nine tackles along with a forced fumble and a sack. That's one game I'll never forget!

• During our game against Puyallup High, I listened from my safety position as the quarterback made an audible, which resulted in a quick pitch to the outside for a first down. The next time I heard him make that same call, from the same offensive formation, I had a huge grin on my face. When the ball was snapped, I jumped across the line of scrimmage and nailed the running back for a big loss. This was especially satisfying for me because I lived in Puyallup, but because of the way the school boundary lines were drawn I was assigned to attend Spanaway Lake High.

• Playing with Adam was a special treat. We both bleached our hair blond, something of a trend among young football players at the time. I still kid him about the time he stepped on my hand. I was a gunner on our punt cover team, and I was on the ground after getting kicked and knocked on my butt when Adam ran past me and stomped on my right hand. It was a cold and rainy day, so my hand swelled up and really hurt. My brother claims he doesn't remember this happening, but I know better. My teammates and I also would give him crap about all the passes he dropped from his tight end position. Adam would try to set the record straight, insisting that only six balls were thrown to him all season and that he caught five of them.

• At safety I was usually lined up alongside Muckie Foreman, who also led our team as quarterback. I looked up to Muckie, almost idolized him really, but in my yearbook at the end of that school year, when he was going off to play for the University of Montana, Muckie wrote something that really surprised me: "All season long you thought I was teaching you, but you were really teaching me."

I finished the season with 37½ tackles, including two for a loss, along with two forced fumbles and that fumble return for a touchdown. As a running back, I gained 212 yards on 24 carries and four TDs, and I caught four passes for 33 yards and a TD. By no means did I breeze through my first high school season without making mistakes. I made lots of them! I remember one time when one of our cornerbacks and I both got hurdled by a talented wide receiver who ran for a TD. On another play I read screen pass but it turned out to be a fake screen. I got totally burned on that one.

Each time something went wrong, however, I was back up and ready for the next play. I was loving the competition, embracing the opportunity given to me to be out on the field most of the time. I was proud that my teammates were already looking up to me. As my friend Steven recalls, *"Logan was a natural safety because he was smart enough to read the play and instinctive enough to come up and fill. He just 'had it,' you know, the way some players do. Everybody could see that."*

My dad also totally enjoyed my one high school football season. By his own admission, he was one of those loud fans who would not refrain from voicing discontent when he disagreed with an official's call. At one point during the season he was summoned to report to our school principal. I think he was afraid he was going to be barred from the stadium. "You can still come to the games," he was told, "but only if you take the role of filming the action instead of sitting there yelling."

My dad also made it very clear to me that if I didn't earn good enough grades in school, he would not let me play football. That sure motivated me to become the excellent student I was known as at Spanaway Lake High! My dad also supported my dream by sending out multiple letters to college football coaches highlighting my accomplishments as a sophomore. As well as playing offense and defense, I was also a fixture on special teams. I was voted our team's Rookie of the Year.

After football season was over, I played basketball for Spanaway Lake High. I had always loved playing hoops and once believed that was going to be my sports ticket to bigger things. By now, football had taken center stage, but I stuck with basketball to stay physically active through the winter while keeping the competitive fire burning.

When spring rolled around, it was time for one of my favorite parts of playing varsity football: weight training. I know some players barely tolerate or can't stand offseason workouts. They just want to be on the field on game day. But I absolutely loved spring workouts. Before I got to high school, I didn't have much experience with weight-lifting and other physical training. In junior high we did have a PE class where we would lift weights sometimes, but I didn't really put much into it. It was just experimenting with free weights and a universal. My exposure changed dramatically when I became part of our high school team's summer training program before my sophomore year began.

I still remember how Ro would crank up his favorite workout music, the hard rock band AC/DC. I pushed myself big-time because I wanted to prove to Muckie and the other rising seniors that I could keep up with them. My max power clean was about 255 pounds. I would clean with my buddy Brandon. For our own musical accompaniment we turned to a love song, *If You're Not the One* by Daniel Bedingfield. If you listen to the lyrics, you would have a hard time imagining how this song could inspire kids to throw themselves into weight-lifting, but we just went nuts when we would hear it. "Let's do this!" Brandon would yell. Ro never let us do what are called "max squats" because of the high risk of injury, so we'd do "projected squats." That means you do a set with as many reps as possible until failure. Most guys could do three to six reps of their highest weight, but I had strong legs. I had 300 pounds on and could do 10 reps without assistance, although on the 10th rep I would nearly pass out from exhaustion. With projected squats, doing 10 reps at 300 pounds roughly equates to doing one rep at a max of 400. As far as I knew, that was pretty heavy lifting for an incoming sophomore.

So in the spring after my sophomore season, I was ready for more … and Ro was ready to give it out. He introduced a new workout that would really push our limits, something he picked up at a clinic run by Boyd Epley, the famed strength coach who helped the University of Nebraska Cornhuskers become a college football powerhouse in the '90s. The workout regimen is called the Metabolic Circuit. As Ro explained it to me, the circuit stimulates muscle mass and also a loss of fat mass in a short amount of time, basically forcing your body to make a change. You do squats, quads, hands, chest, back, arms, triceps, etc. The challenging part is you do 10 exercises fast in a row: Do the exercise for 30 seconds, rest 90 seconds, then do the exercise again. We did the circuit twice a week for six weeks. Some of the players would be vomiting before the end of the circuit, and many who began the six-week program did not make it through to the end. It was an optional workout because, as Ro told us, "It's not for the faint of heart." Naturally I jumped right on it … and I loved it!

Sure, it was rough. We were doing curls with 20 pounds of weight. You could barely do three before you were falling over. It was insane, really. But like Ro says, it forces your body to make a change, and the change in my body was a welcome one. I gained about 30 pounds, mostly muscle, and my speed and strength definitely increased at the same time. I knew I would be even more explosive on the field for my junior season. My teammates weren't going to call me Gumby anymore!

This new, intense workout continued on past the end of the school year in June '03. Since my dad and Sally were both working, and I didn't yet have my driver's license, I had no way of getting to school. No problem: I borrowed a neighbor's bike and bicycled seven miles to school, completed the Metabolic Circuit, then hopped back on the bike and pedaled seven miles back home. That pushed my body's limits even further.

At home, my dad had been doing his part to support my physical development all along. He had put me on Creatine, the supplement that had become extremely popular among college and pro athletes for its ability to build muscle mass. Every day when I would get home from doing the Metabolic Circuit, he would have a protein shake waiting for me. I still make the same kind of protein shake today. The drink provides about 2,000 calories with a combination of chocolate protein, chocolate milk, ice cream, and a banana, and it tastes like a dessert. Every morning during the school year, my dad would make me a breakfast of steak and eggs, with potatoes. I remember hearing Ro say, "You got to work it, rest it, and feed it." I was doing all of that and more.

Becoming bigger, faster, and stronger was definitely helping me zoom in on my goal of playing major college football. I wasn't too small now, and there was no doubt I would continue to work out at this rugged pace. As Ro would say, "You're the first one in the workout room and the last one out." At home after school or on weekends, I would often work out on my Dad's Bowflex training machine. I was imagining myself beefing up to 215 pounds or more before my high school career was over.

I also had been voted team captain during the offseason after my sophomore year, an unusual honor for any player who was not a rising senior. I had always been a captain in whatever sport I played. A lot of that had to do with my hard work and the way I would listen to the coach and do whatever he asked me to do, without asking why. You just tell me how long I had to run or how far I needed to jump, and I would do it.

I wasn't the vocal type as a team leader, preferring to lead more by my actions. But I remember an incident at summer camp at Central Washington University before the injury. One of the sophomores, along with a few of his buddies, found some beer and drank it all in the dorms. Coach Ro gathered all the captains together and asked what we should do about this transgression. We made it clear that the leader of this escapade had to be held accountable and that he should be kept in the dorm for the next day of camp. He took his punishment well, and the day after sitting out he showed his greatest effort yet on the field. That was the spirit in which I expected to continue to lead.

The recruitment letter from Boise State fueled my hopes and dreams. Dan Hawkins was the head coach then, and Chris Petersen was his offensive coordinator. This was the period in which Boise State was on the verge of making a surprising splash among the nation's elite teams. The Broncos had just gone 12-1 in '02. By '06, when Chris had become head coach, they were an unbeaten team making headlines with a stunning 43-42 Tostitos Fiesta Bowl triumph over the University of Oklahoma, winning the game on a two-point conversion with the old-fashioned Statue of Liberty play. Had I gone on to enroll at Boise State and earned a place on the team, I would have been right in the middle of all of that.

Back at Harborview Medical Center in Seattle, I was spending most of my time lying on a hospital bed. I was kept in intensive care for six or seven days. Everything was all so new to me. I had a buzzer that I could push to notify the nurse if I needed pain meds, and I have to admit I really did need those meds when I started to feel the pain from what had happened to me. I had a morphine drip, and every night around 10 p.m., I would start to feel weird. That's when the pain medication would start leaving my body. I was not bashful about ringing that buzzer.

"I'm not feeling good; I need some more meds," I would say. When they did the drip it felt like a cold sensation going through my arm. Then, when the sensation came up to my shoulder area, I could feel some kind of pop and my whole body started to feel warm. I began to understand what it feels like for people who get addicted to drugs. It was just a feeling of ecstasy. I made a mental note to myself: Once I got out of the hospital, no more pain meds.

I could deal with the pain. All I really was interested in was feeling any degree of movement or sensation in my body. Immediately after the surgery, I had no feeling from my chest down, just like that doctor said would be true … forever. At least I could feel the top of my shoulders and my neck, and a little bit of my arms. I could even pick up my shoulders a little bit, too. But a couple of days after the surgery I was encouraged to notice that I could feel a little farther down. That was something.

My family and friends hardly left my bedside, or so it seemed, and they were keeping their eyes out for any positive signs, too. I'm pretty sure Jordyn found a way to spend the night at least once, no doubt breaking hospital rules. My dad and Sally were both given time off from work and were driving back and forth from Puyallup every day, usually with Brandon and Steven and a couple of my other teammates with them. "We'd stay until the end of visiting hours, go home, get up, and do it all over again," Steven recalls. "We ate a lot of strawberry ice cream at that hospital." The player from Redmond High that I had tried to destroy with the hit that caused my injury even stopped by to see how I was doing. That really meant a lot to me; he didn't have to do that.

My teammates were very clear about how they were going to approach me in my almost motionless state. The first day they visited me, Steven broke the ice, joking about the halo on my head. "It is what it is, bro; we're not gonna feel sorry for you," he said. "We're just here to help you." It wasn't until years later that Brandon admitted that when they weren't in front of me in my room, they cried a time or two about what had happened.

"But you never cried," Brandon insisted when we were remembering back to those first days.

"Yeah, I did cry," I said, "just not when you were there."

Yes, the reality of what had happened did begin to seep in through the cracks of my "no big deal" wall. It would usually happen late at night, when visiting hours were over and the guys and my dad and Coach Ro and Jordyn had gone back home. Alone in my quiet room, except for the nurses who would come and go, I had my down moments. I never, ever asked "Why me?" but I did allow myself to ask many other questions about what my life was to be. I was scared.

"Will I ever play football again?" I asked my dad once during that first week at Harborview.

"Well, you'll have something to do with the sport," he said carefully.

"Will I ever walk again?" I asked.

"Yeah," he said, "you will."

I was asking some of the same kinds of questions during quiet moments with Jordyn, and her support, confidence, and encouragement were unwavering. Ro also exuded a firm confidence. Just as I always knew he had my back on the football field, I was just as sure that he had my back now. It was Ro who first presented me with the words, and the philosophy, that would go on to become my rallying cry for facing life with a spinal cord injury.

It was late one evening, as I recall, close to the end of visiting hours.

"There's a quote I know, and I want you to think about it," Ro said. "Life is 10 percent what happens to you and 90 percent how you react to it."

"I appreciate that, Coach," I said.

Later that night, when one of those down moments began to descend on me, I thought about that quote. I started to see how it fit my situation perfectly. What had just happened to me, suffering a spinal cord injury that in one instant had taken away my dream of playing college and pro football and had left me with mountains to climb to ever potentially walk again, was only 10 percent of my life. But 90 percent of my life would be shaped and molded by how I was going to react to this unexpected accident. Was I going to let it drag me down, leaving me in a constant state of feeling sorry for myself, bitter about each and every limitation and new direction this injury would force me to go in? Or was I somehow, some way, going to take a more positive approach, finding the inner resources to embrace and appreciate everything that was good about the life I was leading while summoning the strength and commitment to tackle the challenges that came with this transformative injury?

The choice of how I was going to fill in that 90 percent of life was going to be all mine, and I had a pretty good idea which path I would be following. I may have been only a teenager, but I knew something about myself. I didn't get to be a hard-hitting safety groomed for a bright future in football despite weighing 155 pounds as a high school sophomore with a negative approach to life … and the possibilities of how to make it the best it could possibly be.

CHAPTER THREE

The "Funnest" Summer

THERE ARE MANY GREAT THINGS about being part of a high school football team. There's the camaraderie that builds from spending so much time together, and weathering the good times and bad times on the field as brothers. There's the hard work toward a common goal, not only trying to win but also representing your school in the best way you can. There's the joking and ribbing you get when you know each other well and you're all committed to keeping everybody's spirits light. There's the passionate support you both give and receive, from your coaches and from one another, for developing as players and young men.

As the summer of 2003 went on, my Spanaway Lake High football team added another dimension to what teammates will do for one another. They demonstrated that when one player suffers a major injury and is confined mostly to a wheelchair in a hospital, where he needs to relearn even the most simple and basic tasks of life, the team will be right there with him every inch of the way. And in my case, the team I still belonged to showed its willingness not just to be there but also to show up with the kind of dedication, enthusiasm, and craziness that only high school football players could truly understand and appreciate. I will be forever grateful for what the Spanaway Lake Sentinels did for me during those days when I had to come to grips with the reality that I would never be out there on the field playing the game of football again.

My teammates made the commitment to this off-field mission soon after I was moved from Harborview Medical Center in Seattle to the in-patient Rehabilitation Program at Good Samaritan Hospital in Puyallup, which was the town I still lived in and a short drive from Spanaway. Puyallup was much easier to get to than Seattle for all the important people in my life: My girlfriend Jordyn, my family, my teammates. Also, with school still out for summer, most of the guys had time on their hands. I guess I sort of became their "summer job."

I got very used to having 30 or 40 people in and out of, and all around, my hospital room. Even my room number fit in with our team approach. I was assigned to Room 23, which was so close to my Spanaway Lake uniform number 22 that I always looked upon it as being Room 22. My jersey number 22 decorated the windows and walls of my room, along with all the get-well cards and letters. I quickly grew accustomed to the presence of my teammates, and the other patients and staff had no choice.

"Your crowd was a little intimidating at first, but we got used to them," my primary physical therapist, Donna Meyer, admitted to me much later. She was smiling when she said that … I think.

"We could see they were just there to support you, to watch you do your exercises and give you a hard time if they felt you could be trying harder. But they were never really disruptive," she explained. "They understood the seriousness of what was going on and respected the environment you were in, as well as the needs of the other patients. We never had to say, 'Hey guys, get out of here.' As therapists, we recognize that the situation patients like you are in just sucks, but then you have this great support system to make it easier. So whatever helps, we're going to use it."

Donna and the entire staff of therapists, doctors, and nurses at Good Sam took on the hardest work: trying to help me get my life back on the right footing. They were down there in the trenches, teaching me and guiding me toward an understanding of how I was going to adjust to living with a spinal cord injury. Just like in football, you have to start by mastering the basics: getting out of bed, sitting upright in a chair, trying to get your clothes on and off without help, figuring out how to control your bowels, and just get on and off the toilet. Then you've also got to learn to feed yourself and, with the help of occupational therapists in the kitchen training area, you even get to practice using a microwave and making a sandwich. I really struggled with the mayonnaise, which totally ticked me off! These lessons were invaluable in beginning to glimpse what it would take to be independent with where I was, and what I had, to call upon in my life to that point.

Donna also taught me that if you want to learn to walk someday, the first step is to learn how to stand. That's important to rebuild bone density. Then they explore whether there is something else you can progress to. So they had me up on the parallel bars, with two or three of them huddled close by to assist me. Then they would experiment with various devices to support movement, including an exercise where they would put a big belt around my waist and have one therapist pull me forward while another one held my shoulders back from behind.

The spirit in which they help spinal cord patients at Good Sam is that you've got to learn to use what function and ability you do have. Then, if and when you gain more movement and ability, you learn to use that as well. Fortunately for me, I was beginning to get more movement back in my body much faster than anyone had anticipated.

One of the first positive signs showed up one night in the shower. I was a long way from being able to shower by myself at that time, which meant one of the nurses was in there assisting me. You can bet that's a pretty awkward thing for a 16-year-old boy. Anyway, I was sitting in the shower chair when all of a sudden my left leg twitched.

"Did I really just do that?" I said to the nurse.

"I don't know," she responded, "but try to do it again."

So I focused with total concentration on that area of my left leg ... and it moved a little bit again! I must have done it five or six times in a row. "It must be me," I thought. "I'm really making my leg move."

When I got out of the shower, I grabbed my phone and called Jordyn.

"Holy crap, babe; I just moved my leg!" I shouted.

"What? Seriously!? That's amazing!" she said.

"I know! I thought it was a twitch but then I tried to make it move again myself and it did it!"

"Oh my gosh, Logan, I am so proud of you!"

When we hung up, I called my father and shared the exciting news with him, too. I felt like I had kicked a--! It was the same kind of thrill I used to get from doing the toughest workouts with the football team, only this time, the stakes seemed somehow higher. As news spread around the staff attending to me, one of the nurses said, "Wow, you are a miracle!"

So almost right away, I was demonstrating that things were not going to be as bad as those doctors thought they were going to be. The staff at Good Sam explained to me later that they always knew it was at least possible that I would regain some function, eventually. Still, when I had come in with no movement at all, they didn't want to instill any false hopes by talking about what *could* happen someday. And they had no crystal ball to tell them what would be. No one does.

In my perspective, I had no doubt that my ability to regain any movement in my leg could be at least partially attributed to how strong I was before the accident. During all those rigorous workouts at school, my legs were always the strongest part of my body. I also remembered the neck stretches we used to do. You would be on all fours and put your head down, and then one of your teammates would place his hand on top of our head. As you pushed up, your teammate pushed down. So I had a new reason to be thankful for that hard work I had been doing all spring and early summer, and for the guys who were right there with me to urge me on … just as they are now.

Another positive sign emerged from a little "test" one of the doctors was giving me. Every day, when I wasn't looking at his hands, he would sneakily pinch my foot to see if I would feel it and respond by shifting my glance toward him. Apparently I failed his test a bunch of times, but then one day when he pinched me, I immediately shot my gaze toward the scene of his action.

"Oh, did you feel that?" he asked innocently.

"I think so," I said.

So he moved on to tougher "questions" on the test, each day pinching me in more and more places. I was feeling the pinch a bit more here, a bit more there. As is often true with spinal cord patients, the feelings were coming back before the movement. I started feeling all over my arms and legs. It soon became clear to the Good Sam staff that after initially trusting the diagnosis that I had a complete spinal cord injury, which means your spinal cord is completely severed and you have no feeling and no movement from a certain point on down, I actually had an *incomplete* spinal cord injury. I *did* have feeling in many parts of my body below my chest. I was very slowly regaining at least some degree of movement.

Of course, since I had more to use, that meant I was going to be expected to use it, and sure enough, within only four months after the injury occurred, with extremely hard work and strenuous exercise, I was able to stand up! I was only able to stand with the assistance of the therapists though, and it was inside the parallel bars, as they would help lift me out of the chair, and once standing I had a tight grip on the bars so I wouldn't fall over. It was very hard to stay balanced, and was weird to stand again, but it was such an amazing feeling and gave me a surge of excitement to know that the road to recovery progressed one step farther.

Once I gained the strength to stand up, I moved beyond those parallel bars to trying some steps in the corridors. Corrine was my trainer in this endeavor, and while Donna would use humor to keep things going with me, Corrine was all business. I would move forward with the use of hand grips or a walker with wheels and tennis balls on the bottom. At one point she had me try walking with a cane. She would march me from the therapy room to the front entrance of the rehab center, and by the time I reached that destination I swear that I was sweating more than I ever did when I pushed myself through Coach Ro's workouts.

Those Good Sam therapists could be hard on me, which I needed and liked. When Donna informed me that it was time to learn how to sit cross-legged, and I asked how I was going to do that, she just said, "Figure it out." When they urged me to walk down the exercise stairs, I could not figure out how to support myself in walking down the four steps facing forward. So I simply walked down facing backward. I admit, there were days when I just didn't want to rise up and sign on to my next rehab workout, no matter what it was or how much would be expected of me. That's where having my football team around me made such a big difference.

The prevailing attitude of Brandon, Steven, and all my other friends sounded something like this: "Come on, dude, stop being a baby. Just move your leg (or do whatever it was that was called for during an exercise)." Just like in the training room at Spanaway Lake High, they weren't going to let me slack off. They related to me with nothing but positivity, and that's just what I wanted. I hated being treated like I was disabled, or being handled like I was a fragile piece of glass.

As Steven remembers it, "Other people would be saying things like, 'Oh, it will be OK, Logan,' but we'd say, 'Get you're a-- up and get going!' During physical therapy, your brothers would be right there in your ear. We never changed how we talked to you just because of the injury. I bet none of the other patients knew what to make of us. They're thinking, this guy is paralyzed and they're all yelling at him."

The positive encouragement definitely helped me do what I needed to do, and their playful way of being around me made me feel like I still had a sense of continuity in my life. They started bringing in Otter Pops for us to share between workouts.

For those who didn't grow up with them, Otter Pops are those fruit juice freezies in a clear plastic tube. We used to devour them by the boxful during breaks between games when we were younger, and as we enjoyed this familiar treat again at Good Sam, the guys would lament about how much they missed the strawberry ice cream at Harborview. They also set up a Nerf basketball hoop in my hospital room and insisted that I take my turn in trying to shoot baskets. Well, I could barely move one arm, so my shooting form consisted of flicking my left hand a bit sideways and pitching the ball a short distance. Out of 10 shots from close range, I would be lucky to sink one! It didn't matter. We just laughed and kept on finding more ways to have a little fun. When the guys brought in our favorite video games and recognized that I could not manage a regular high-five to celebrate a peak moment, they improvised: We did gentle backhand high-fives.

Wheelchairs became a frequent source of amusement. I had already shown them how I would speed around the hallways in my power wheelchair and then, at the last moment as I approached Room 23, I'd turn hard left and drift into the room. My teammates figured since I had to spend almost all my time in my wheelchair, they should start spending time in wheelchairs, too.

Steven had a little previous experience in this form of transportation after suffering a pelvis injury a good while earlier. Soon he was demonstrating the proper technique to do a wheelie, and the other guys were of course eager to try it out. For them, though, it wasn't enough just to maneuver around my room or take a short spin down the corridors of Good Sam. Just as with any of our football activities, they had their eyes open for a tougher test. Somehow they got hold of a few of those rickety old wheelchairs the hospital still had around and wheeled them outside the main entrance, where they took advantage of the steep downhill slope toward the parking garage to see what kind of speed they could ramp up to. Those little front wheels would be shaking so violently, I'd swear they were going to break and they'd go tumbling down the hill!

Little pranks like that prevented me from fixating on the unknowns still in front of me. As Brandon reminded me, even if I had wanted to be depressed, they wouldn't let me. So they just kept ragging on me while I was trying to walk, with remarks like, "Dude, stop dragging along like that and pick up your damn legs. It's not that hard!" Obviously they knew that trying to move my legs, or to complete any of my rehab exercises, was actually very hard. Yet by sprinkling a bit of humor on the situation, they made all my tasks not only more bearable but also more *enjoyable*. Of course, they could be absolutely merciless at times: picking at my arms or flicking me, just to see what I was going to do about it, or blowing baby powder toward me and then laughing, "Ha ha, gotcha—white face!" I soaked it all in.

Apparently my dad encouraged the guys to act a little crazy around me. "He told us that if we were going to be around Logan and just mope, he would throw us out," Steven recalls. Soon my teammates worked out a daily routine where they would hang out with me for several hours, and then leave Good Sam and head right to school for football training.

So my teammates were totally in sync with my new 10 and 90 spirit: *Life is 10 percent what happens to you and 90 percent how you react to it*. Every moment they were around me, they were reminding me that the way to react to this injury was to remember that life was still going to be about trying your best at whatever it was you were challenged to do, that I was still the same Logan, that I still had friends around me to share whatever was going on, and that I still needed to take time to have fun.

Jordyn and my family were just as supportive in urging me to maintain this positive outlook. It was difficult for my family to get used to me needing more of their physical assistance, and it was certainly hard for me to accept needing that kind of help! My dad was always ready to urge me to go a little farther each time I would try to walk with some kind of aid. Since he had been a high-level collegiate swimmer, he was especially interested in the therapy pool at Good Sam and was quick to suggest that I be allowed to try it. When I got in the pool, my dad would be right in there with me, helping me move around in the water and just feel some feelings in my legs a little bit.

Jordyn's mom, Susie, also had been urging me to get in the water. However, when the time came for the staff to actually bring me into the pool, she began to get just a little nervous about how I would be able to stay afloat. Recognizing her anxiety, my Good Sam team directed her to get right into the pool with me, which Susie was happy to do. I already considered Susie part of my family, so her support was very important to me.

Getting in the water gave me a feeling of freedom that I really needed. I wasn't sitting in a wheelchair, lying in a bed, or struggling to take a step with the support of others all around me. In the water, my body was actually able to move around. I heard that President Roosevelt had that same feeling of freedom when he would get out of his wheelchair and immerse himself in the mineral springs in Warm Springs, Georgia.

It was also liberating to get out of the hospital once in a while, which my family helped make possible. On my first outing, we actually went to a movie: *Pirates of the Caribbean*. Then we made an important visit to my grandma, my dad's mom, who was living in a retirement home. Grandma had not been doing well for some time, but on that Sunday visit she was in the best of spirits I had seen her in for years. She was aware of who we were and what we were doing, and I'm sure she felt empathy for me, seeing me in a wheelchair. She understood what it meant to have limited physical ability.

When it was time for us to leave, I said, "I love you, Grandma. See you later." The next day she passed away. It was as if she had been given one more day to see us all the way she used to, before age had taken its toll.

On another outing, Jordyn and I had a picnic in Bradley Lake Park, a nice spot in the center of Puyallup with a 12-acre lake, picnic areas, ball fields, a playground, and walking trails. I loved breathing the fresh air and seeing other people active. I have to admit I didn't much care for the motorized wheelchair I was using at the time, and Jordyn probably wasn't too happy when I accidentally ran over her toes when she was wearing her flip-flops! As time went on, I would find that I was more comfortable with a manual chair that I could power with my own arms.

Jordyn stayed near me in the hospital every second she possibly could, every day, consistently pushing me to fight, to believe in possibilities. She would go with me to my counseling sessions, and she would root me on during physical therapy, speaking firm words of encouragement if I showed any sign of backing down from any challenge. Jordyn understood what I would not allow the others to see: I still got scared. Yes, my injury was an incomplete spinal cord injury rather than a complete spinal cord injury. That meant I had some feeling and some movement in parts of my body below my chest. But the long-term prognosis was still far from rosy. I had mountains to climb to claim any degree of independence. The wheelchair was going to remain a fixture in my life.

I was determined to do everything I possibly could to walk again, but I recognized that I really did not know what my life was going to be, and how I would deal with the seriousness of my injury. I was absolutely going to infuse every bit of positivity that I could into that 90 percent of how I reacted to living with a spinal cord injury, but that didn't mean that I would never have a dark moment. My strength and faith were going to be tested. That was just part of the deal. There were times late at night at Good Sam when I would be lying on my bed watching TV and a few tears would spill out. I still didn't ask, "Why me?" but, while all these big changes in my life were sinking in, I might find myself asking, "What if?"

Fortunately, having Jordyn, my family, and my teammates pulling for me with every ounce of their being just made sure that those dark moments never lasted very long, and that each time I got even a little worried, they would be there to boost my spirits and my will. How could I ever sulk with so many people who cared for me right there to share the experience and to root for me to make the best of it I possibly could?

They believed. They pushed me to fight. They made sure the words "no" and "I can't" would almost never enter my vocabulary.

With Jordyn, the injury had thrown a huge challenge into the heart of our relationship. Yet I knew I didn't have to ever worry about her ability to rise to that challenge. Here's how she remembers that time:

"In many ways it felt like Logan and I grew up together through his injury. The way I looked at being together was that you were either all in, or you're not. I was all in. In many ways, being around Logan during those days made me appreciate him even more. Seeing him have to relearn how to brush his teeth or how to dress himself, I saw his vulnerability. And sometimes when he was doing his physical exercises, he would be OK with failing—for the moment. But he would always be right back at it and keep trying. It was like I was seeing the real Logan coming out more. Before the injury he was always the cool football captain, and nothing ever bothered him. Now he didn't have to be that way. He was very determined, but he also could be scared of

what was going to happen. He realized he didn't have to be strong all the time.

"For me, my motherly instinct began to come out more in doing little things to help take care of him. We were both control freaks, and we both had to learn to let go more. When I learned how to help put in his catheter, I just looked at it as, 'This is business; it's what we have to do. This is you now, and I have to do this for you, but it's not you all the time.' We both had played sports and taken that very seriously, but now we had to realize there was more to life than sports. We could bring in our competitive nature when we were doing things like helping him master how to use a fork, but we found other things we had in common too. We were both in this together. I was never embarrassed to be around him in his wheelchair. I was just becoming more and more proud of who he was and how he was living his life."

The staff at Good Sam also fully devoted themselves to helping me rise to the challenges in front of me. They gave me everything they had, and when I began to show signs of feeling and movement in more parts of my body, they hit the ground running in trying to encourage me to take steps on my own. Donna told me once that it was actually very surprising to have a patient like me who was beginning to engage in walking exercises during in-patient therapy. I remember one time she pointed out another patient who was walking very gracefully, with just a little support from a cane. "Twenty years ago he broke his neck, too," she explained. Donna told me later she never remembered me having a bad day, that I was always eager to try the next thing. The staff sometimes called me Superman and, when I was leaving the hospital, they presented me with an all-white T-shirt with blue in the middle and the writing, "Superman #22." One day Donna even asked me for my autograph. She was smiling when she explained, "I just have a feeling you're going to do big things someday."

I had no way of knowing what "big things" I might ever be able to do in my life back then. I only knew that they wouldn't be about making a hard tackle and having my friends see me on ESPN. But these friends, my loyal teammates, were just as committed to watching me grow and achieve things in my life now as when I was standing side by side with them in the training room or on the football field getting ready for the next big play.

"People are like tubes of toothpaste: When you squeeze, what's inside comes out," Brandon was saying once while remembering those times in the rehab center of Good Samaritan Hospital in the summer of '03. "For 90 percent of people in the world who went through something like Logan did, they would probably react in a much more negative way. But Logan just had this maturity, this determination to stay positive. We were just there to do our part in helping him keep it up. And we had fun. You have to laugh; life is too short. I mean, we were even fighting over who was going to take care of his pee bags. Looking back at it now, I have to say it was one of the funnest summers ever."

It may sound strange to call what others would consider hell as "fun." But having an ever-evolving wave of my best friends and my family by my side every day, and doing things together that were challenging but also sometimes crazy, really did make the whole experience fun. I mean, how could you not laugh when you watch your friends do wheelies in wheelchairs or go speeding down the hill of the parking lot outside your hospital? How could you not crack up when they blow baby powder in your face? How could you not smile inside when someone like Steven looks at your walker and says, "You don't need this s---. Just walk. If you fall, fall forward. I'll catch you."

Yeah, it was a fun summer all right, a summer that I will never forget, and one of the major reasons I am as positive as I am in my day-to-day life today.

CHAPTER FOUR

The Turkey Bowl

ALL MEMORABLE SUMMERS HAVE TO come to an end, and that summer of '03 was no exception. After all my hard work with the dedicated staff in rehab, all the love and caring I received from my family, and all the laughs I shared with my teammates at Good Samaritan Hospital, I was going to be released from the in-patient program and set free to go back to my life. I didn't know exactly what to expect, but I was certain of one thing: I was no longer going to be able to play sports. And from the time I was big enough to hold a ball in my hands, sports had been pretty much my whole life.

I inherited a love for playing sports from my dad. Dan Seelye enjoyed all kinds of sports, but his first love was swimming. Growing up in Tacoma, as the son of an electrician, he remembers going to a lake with a diving board when he was 7 years old. He really wanted to jump off that diving board, but my grandfather told him, "If you want to jump off that board, you need to learn how to swim first." So he sent my dad to their local YMCA, with its pool down in the dungeon-like environment of the basement. He soon learned to swim well enough to dive off that diving board, and a whole lot more. Beginning his competitive swimming early, he participated in a swim team through Pacific Lutheran University. Then one day my grandfather surprised him by driving him to the prestigious Tacoma Swim Club and announcing that he was going to be training there under the direction of high-profile coach Dick Hannula. During his long, outstanding career, Coach Hannula coached the U.S. National swim team for many years and managed the U.S. team at the 1984 and '88 Olympics. My dad was learning from the best!

Before he zeroed in on swimming, my dad had participated in other sports. There was one sport he especially wanted to play but was forbidden to engage in: football. The way he tells the story, he was being examined by his family's pediatrician while in junior high school. The doctor made a pronouncement: Dan's bones were too soft to play football. My grandfather accepted this verdict, and that was the end of my father's football dreams. Ironically, he would still play tackle football with the neighborhood kids at a local field—with no pads! But he was not allowed to play for his junior high school football team. He turned to wrestling instead, and you have to wonder how a doctor could decide that his bones were strong enough for that sport but could not hold up to football. Anyway, he got as far as his high school junior varsity wrestling team when my grandfather said it was time to choose: wrestling or swimming. That's when he got serious about swimming. Training at the Tacoma Swim Club was not cheap, and my father gives credit to my grandparents for the sacrifices they made to make it happen. At one point my grandfather even became president of the Tacoma Swim Club and my grandmother served as secretary, typing the results of the swim meets.

The backstroke was my dad's top event. Swimming for the Wilson High School swim team that also was guided by Coach Hannula, Dan Seelye ranked third in the state in the 200 backstroke as a sophomore, then second as a junior, and first as a senior. He also excelled in the 200 IM (individual medley) and was part of a relay team for Wilson when it won a high school state championship. After earning a swimming scholarship at the University of Miami and enrolling there, he wound up transferring back home and competing for the University of Puget Sound in Tacoma. He set national records in the 100 and 200 backstroke in college and earned an invitation to the

Olympic Trials twice, though he fell short of qualifying. He told me that he would train 11 months a year during his prime competitive swimming period.

With this background, you know my father would encourage his three boys to play sports. My oldest brother Aaron was more of a bookworm and didn't take to sports so much, but my brother Adam, two years older than me, loved to play any game he could from the time he was very young. When I came along, I was just as eager to get in there with him.

I was born on April 1, 1987, which means I was an April Fool's baby. The way the story was told in my family, my mother called my father early that morning and said, "My water broke. It's time." Naturally my dad rushed home, but when he got there my mother was laughing. "April Fools," she said. I doubt he was too happy about having to turn right around and head back to work, and when she called early that evening and insisted it really *was* time, he didn't believe her. He was not going to fall for that April Fool's joke twice! She kept insisting and insisting that she was telling the truth, until he finally understood that she wasn't fooling. I was born at 10:19 p.m. on April Fool's Day.

My dad wanted to name me Andrew, to be the third "A" in the house, but since I also had a cousin named Alyse, my grandmother told my dad that this made for one too many "A" names in the family. So my parents went back to the baby-name drawing board. Around that time, my mother happened to be a big fan of *Logan's Run,* the movie and TV mini-series. That's how I became Logan Seelye.

As a little kid, I definitely knew how to use my status as youngest child in the family to my advantage. Whenever Aaron or Adam did anything remotely bad to me, I would entice them to do it more. Then I'd start crying to attract our parents' attention, and when my brothers got in trouble I felt a wave of satisfaction. As I got a little older, my act wore thin, and Aaron as the oldest was off in his own world.

Adam and I were the sports kids in the house. With my dad's track record in swimming, he naturally wanted Adam and me to give that sport a try. From what he tells us, we did well when we first got in the water and "had the lean bodies and the right build to really kill swimming." But we didn't like being forced to wear those little Speedos and just didn't take to swimming. Reluctantly, my dad let go of any image of raising Olympic swimmers. Instead, he put up a basketball hoop at the cul-de-sac not far from our house. He still brags about making the first long shot from our driveway. My dad would often team up with a neighbor guy to play against Adam and me. I'm sure the two adults beat us in the beginning, but over time we turned the tide. Adam and I both loved basketball. Naturally we were both Seattle SuperSonics' fans, though I wasn't quite old enough to remember when the Sonics played their home games close to us in the Tacoma Dome one season while Key Arena in Seattle was being rebuilt. The Sonics usually reached the playoffs during the '90s, even making it all the way to the NBA finals in '96 before losing to Michael Jordan and the Chicago Bulls in a six-game championship series. They continued to be a powerhouse in the Western Conference for a couple of seasons longer.

Those great Sonics teams were led by Shawn Kemp, a big man who could dunk on anybody, along with point guard Gary Payton and my favorite player, Hersey Hawkins. I kept a life-size poster of Hersey in his #33 Sonics uniform on my bedroom wall from the time I was 5 or 6 years old, along with a poster of Shawn Kemp. As a young kid just learning to play, I mimicked Hersey's free-throw shooting routine: Take three dribbles, spin the ball, bounce into it, and shoot. I didn't quite shoot with Hersey's accuracy, but it was fun to copy a pro basketball player.

My Uncle Scott, my dad's brother, had obtained Sonics season tickets, or knew someone who had them, and through him we were able to attend many games in Seattle. I remember one game when my dad suddenly called out, "Hey, Jack!" When I looked up, I noticed that the guy he was calling to was Jack Sikma, the former Sonics All-Star and member of the 1978-'79

NBA championship Seattle team. No, my dad didn't know Sikma personally, but I was impressed that he felt like he belonged enough to shout out to a superstar. He also urged me to introduce myself to sportscaster Ahmad Rashad once, and I found the nerve to do that.

It was a great time to be growing up as a Seattle sports fan. The Mariners were winning big in baseball in the mid-'90s, and my dad took us to several of their games in the Kingdome. The Mariners had great players like slugger Ken Griffey, Jr., and giant pitcher Randy Johnson, along with likable guys like Jay Buhner, Joey Cora, and Tino Martinez. In 1995, they won 25 of their last 36 games and beat the California Angels in a one-game tie-breaker to clinch their first-ever trip to the playoffs. Their motto was "refuse to lose," and that spirit carried them to a comeback victory over the Yankees in the playoffs. After losing the first two games of the best-of-five series, the Mariners won the next two and then, in the deciding game, they battled back again after falling behind 5-4 in the 11th inning when Edgar Martinez cranked a double that scored the tying run and, in a bold display of base-running, Griffey stormed home from first base with the winning run. They made the playoffs a few more times in the coming years, and slugger Alex Rodriguez began his big-league career in Seattle.

In football, the Seahawks had not yet climbed to the championship-caliber level we have become used to as fans today. During the '90s they had losing or so-so seasons, although they did have a bit more success when Mike Holmgren was coach and even earned a wildcard playoff berth in '99. Believe it or not, I was not as big a fan of football as the other sports while I was growing up. Adam loved watching NFL games, and he broke away from his allegiance to the Seahawks to become a fan of two future Hall of Famers, quarterback Steve Young and wide receiver Jerry Rice, when they were winning championships with the San Francisco 49ers.

Anyway, I was not one of those kids who spent all his time glued to the TV watching sports. Mostly, I just liked to *play* sports. I participated in all of them: basketball, football, T-ball baseball, soccer, and even a little track. We had a good-size backyard, which my dad groomed as a playing field. A designated spot on one of the fences served as a soccer goal, and I remember how he laid out the football field using garden hoses as goal lines. I would play tackle football there sometimes with Adam and his older buddies. I was the young kid, the little guy, but I wouldn't quit when they hit me—and they hit me pretty good. I remember running up against one big guy named Mush and a kid named Nick Marciano, whose great uncle was heavyweight champion boxer Rocky Marciano.

There was a gravel area closer to the house where we would pick up little stones and smack them with tennis racquets high over the fence into our neighbor's property. We would pretend we were Ken Griffey, Jr., hitting a home run to win the game in the bottom of the ninth inning. Whack! When some of those Griffey home runs hit the house across our yard, the neighbor who lived there came storming over to our house to complain. After Dad calmed him down, he just told us to change games for a while until the heat was off.

I was always energetic as a kid. Whatever Adam was doing, I wanted to do it, too. Like most big brothers, Adam was initially annoyed at how I always wanted to tag along. "Stay away," he would say. I didn't listen, of course, and he soon came around to accept my company on the sports trail, wherever it happened to be leading us during any time of year or on any particular day. Adam was always pushing me to get better. When we played in the backyard, he would challenge me not just to catch the football or baseball but also to see how far I could stretch or dive to grab it. He helped me appreciate how to use whatever sports gear we had around. As an example, we kept an old, beat-up leather basketball that anyone looking at would wonder how we could use it. We had learned that when the weather was wet, the grip on that leather ball was far superior to the grip on a regular basketball.

Over time, some of Adam's friends wanted to spend more time engaging in non-sports activities, but Adam wanted to keep playing sports. So he adjusted to playing more with my younger friends. As long as were playing together, we didn't care who the other kids were.

Once in a while, we'd also make time for other activities, such as watching action-oriented TV shows like *Beast Wars,* where animals turned into weapons. And of course we loved video games. I remember the Christmas when I just *had* to have the new Nintendo 64. My brothers and I had asked for it every day for weeks, and on Christmas morning we rushed downstairs expecting to find it under or around the tree. When we couldn't locate it at first, we were all really bummed. Then my dad said, "Wait, what's this?" as he held up a letter from Grandpa. That made Aaron, Adam and me perk up instantly. The letter directed us to three different places until we finally came upon the 64 with all the controls and games we were yearning for. My parents always tried to make things interesting for us at Christmas. Sometimes, instead of labeling the presents with our names, they would use code letters to represent our names. So we had to first decipher the code before we could figure out which presents were for each of us.

I began school at Pioneer Valley Elementary in Spanaway. After my parents moved me to private school for a couple of years, I returned to Pioneer Valley for fifth and sixth grade. I was playing every sport that had a youth program, including the Puyallup Roughriders peewee football team. I actually began on the *89ers*, which was just for kids ages 8 to 9. I was faster than most of the other kids and played running back and linebacker. On offense, my favorite play was a double-reverse, where I'd start on one side of the field, fake like I was running outside after the snap, then cut back toward the middle of the field where the other running back had already taken the hand-off and had begun motoring one way. He would then hand it off to me as I was running in the opposite direction. I'd be chugging along at a full sprint when I got the ball, and those defenders trying to turn around and catch me had no chance! We ran this play successfully many times. My dad still has videos of the touchdowns I scored on that double-reverse.

I also remember when my dad bought arm guards for me to address my chronic complaints about my arms hurting from getting helmets smacked into them so often. These were black, padded forearm pads that covered the outside of my arm from my wrist all the way up to my elbow. They were kind of bulky, but they did the job. Not only did they protect my arms, but they also helped me break tackles when I covered up the ball with both arms and rammed into my opponent.

One tradition that began when I was very young and continued for several years was our neighborhood Turkey Bowl games. As you can guess, these were games we played on Thanksgiving Day. I can remember when the tradition began, with Dad and his friends joining in. Eventually, it was just us kids. You have to understand, this was too big a deal for our backyard field with the garden hoses to mark the end zones. We had to play on a *real* football field. So we would get up at 6 or 7 a.m., get dressed, and go out on a scouting mission to find one of the school football fields that was not going to have a school game played on it that day. When we found our field, it was game on! These were intense games, especially on those Thanksgiving mornings that presented wet and rainy game conditions. As we always said, the muddier the better. We'd play hard until 10:00 or 10:30 a.m., then trudge home and clean up before sitting down to turkey and all the fixings. By late afternoon or early evening, we would be fast asleep. To me, this was the perfect way to spend Thanksgiving.

As much as I enjoyed football in those younger years, basketball was really my sport back then. As a third-grader, I earned a place on Adam's fifth-grade rec team. As I remember it, we were the two best players on the team. I was very quick and could steal the ball from anyone. Of course, when I tried to convert my steals into layups, I would be moving so fast the ball would sometimes clank off the backboard and bounce way out toward mid-court. I played point guard and continued to refine my Hersey Hawkins free-throw shooting form.

By the time I entered Cedarcrest Junior High School in seventh grade, I was quick to sign up for basketball and football, although I wasn't so sure about playing baseball. One of my close friends, Spencer Jones, ran track, and he talked me into doing it with him. Track and baseball season overlapped, so by deciding to run track I didn't play baseball, and it was a good idea as I enjoyed running around and trying a new sport. I competed in the 100 meter, the 400 meter, the 400 meter relay team, and I even did the 110 meter hurdles. My best time in the 400m event was 56 seconds, which I thought was hot stuff until I discovered that Olympic athletes could run it in under 47 seconds. I actually had a lisp back in the day, and I struggled pronouncing the letter "s," so when it came time to do the check-in after the events I always had to have a buddy with me to help pronounce and spell my last name as it usually sounded like I was saying "Feelye" instead of "Seelye." As you could imagine, it was quite frustrating and embarrassing having a speech impediment. I can remember in elementary school I used to get teased about it, and I even went home crying one day because I struggled so hard spelling "Mississippi" out loud during a spelling bee.

After running track in seventh and eighth grade, I decided to go back to baseball for my ninth-grade year, and it was a bad decision! I can't say that I was very good that year. In fact, I was terrible. I played mostly right field and had maybe one base hit all season, with most of my at-bats ending up with weak pop-ups. I mainly did it because I wanted to hang out with my other friends who played baseball, so even though I was awful I had a lot of fun! Needless to say, I stuck with football and basketball as my main sports. I played on the school teams and in the rec leagues, and I was thrilled when Adam got to help coach one of my basketball teams.

After years of hanging out with Adam's friends, I began making more friends of my own through sports. Playing at Cedarcrest helped me to get to know Steven, the friend who later became one of my weight-training buddies in high school. In elementary school we butted heads because while I was at Pioneer Valley, Steven attended Clover Creek Elementary in Tacoma. But in junior high, we became very close friends and discovered our common love for sports. In many ways, we seemed like the same kind of people. We would laugh over the years about how Steven played forward in basketball at Cedarcrest but switched to point guard at Spanaway Lake High, while I played point guard at Cedarcrest but was moved to forward in high school.

We had some "glory days" memories. In basketball, our summer league rec team, the Chargers, made up mostly of players about 5'5" to 5'10", were always getting beat by the Jets, whose players all seemed to be 6'2" or 6'3". I mean, they just towered over us. One season we got together in the locker room before a game against the big, bad Jets and said, "It doesn't matter how many times they beat us. It doesn't matter how big they are. We're gonna win this time!" And we did. It was all will and determination.

I already mentioned some of our football exploits at Cedarcrest Junior High, especially that time we finally defeated our big rival, Bethel, in the game in which I got my bell rung and was too woozy to even know what was going on at the end. Another game that stands out is one against Spanaway Junior High. Steven and I were so competitive that we would sometimes go out to watch the games of our future opponents, to scout them out. While watching Spanaway play against another team, we detected their tendency to begin the game with a trick play. On the day we watched Spanaway, the trick play was a pitch-and-pass, with a running back throwing a pass.

When Spanaway got the ball for the first time in their game against us, Steven and I were talking in the defensive huddle about what we had seen on our scouting mission. "Be on the alert for the pitch-and-pass," we advised. Sure enough, they ran the pitch-and-pass. I read it right from the snap. When that running back faked a run and threw the pass, I was right there to intercept it, dragging my toes on the sidelines to stay in bounds while falling down, reminiscent of a wide receiver scoring a TD on a back-of-the-end-zone fade route. As I was rolling over on the grass, Steven came up out of nowhere and absolutely drilled me on the ground, in a celebratory kind of way. "We knew it!" he yelled. "Can you believe they really tried that play?"

Those were the kinds of moments that kept us fired up and able to keep giving everything we had in every game, every practice. And when there were no games with Cedarcrest or the rec leagues, we'd just get together with friends and play games on our own. Today, you almost never see kids play sports without coaches, uniforms, and everything else that comes with organized sports, but just as it had been for our fathers. we found ways to make sports come alive without any of that stuff.

In our situation, we would combine playing sports with playing video games during marathon weekend sessions of fun and camaraderie. Steven and I would play two-on-two basketball with other friends near Steven's house, and it didn't matter what the weather was. If it was raining, we'd play basketball outside for 30 minutes, come back inside and take off our soaking clothes, then play video games while our clothes dried off. Super Smash Bros. and Mario Tennis were two favorites, and we also liked Xbox games like Halo, where all four of us could play together. It really didn't matter what the game was as long as it was full of action and we could compete against one another. These hoops-and-video-game weekends also launched the tradition of eating Otter Pops. Steven's mom would come in with a big box of 100 or more Otter Pops, and within hours they'd all be devoured. We would take the plastic wrappers they came in and stuff an empty Folgers coffee can to the brim until there was no room left, and we would do this over and over again.

We loved playing different sports so much that we even invented some of our own. One game, OppoBall, was a variation of baseball. We were quite proud of this game. The rules were simple: You play with your opposite hand. So if you throw a baseball with your right hand, you have to switch and use a right-handed glove and throw it with your left hand. You also had to switch the side of the plate you hit with, so if you hit righty you had to switch to lefty and vice-versa. To make things even weirder, we played out at Steven's house, which was on a small hay farm. We had only two bases: home and outfield, and the path to the bases was lined with huge stacks of hay. The goal was to hit the ball as far as possible and make it to the outfield base while running, and usually falling, over the hay. This proved to be quite difficult for both the hitter and the defense as the ball would often get lost in the haystacks! It was an awesome game, not only for the fun of it, but because we all looked so uncoordinated trying to play baseball with our opposite hand!

We'd even create indoor games for those rare times that we absolutely couldn't play outside, or we just didn't want to stray far from our video game consoles. In the basement of Steven's house, eight or 10 mattresses were stacked in one corner. The game worked like this: One guy would climb on the little scooter they kept in there and start riding on the basement's cement floor. The object was to reach the mattresses before your buddies knocked you off the scooter by throwing all kinds of balls at you. Win or lose, the game was a big hit.

I always looked forward to those sports-and-video-games weekends. As soon as school got out on Friday, you would rush home, scramble to get your homework or chores done, then head for Steven's place. If you even tried to fall asleep any time during the weekend, there was a pretty good chance somebody would throw flour in your face to keep you awake, the good ole "antiquing."

It all sounds kind of crazy, and it probably was. Playing football in high school didn't end the craziness. It simply marked an evolution. Sports were still front and center. That was the life I had been living, the life I loved.

Yet, when I checked out of the in-patient rehab program at Good Samaritan Hospital, I knew that it was not the life I was going to be returning to.

CHAPTER FIVE

The Community That Believed

IT WAS A BIG DAY in Spanaway, Washington, our quiet little town just down Pacific Avenue from Tacoma. They called the event "Sentinels Sweep Spanaway for Logan Seelye." All along Pacific Avenue (which is also Route 7) from about 152nd Street to 176th Street, and down the same stretch of B Street running parallel to Pacific, my Spanaway Lake High football teammates, coaches, cheerleaders, families, and friends were spread out to canvass the area. They were holding water buckets, football helmets, or anything else that could take in the quarters, dimes, and dollar bills being generously donated by passers-by from near and far.

It was all for me, and my family, to help offset the steep medical costs related to the treatments for my spinal cord injury. My town, with its population of less than 30,000 people, was stepping up for us big-time!

When I heard that this fund-raising event was being organized while I was still in Good Samaritan Hospital during that summer of '03, I thought they might raise a few hundred bucks. The gesture and the extra money would be greatly appreciated. When they told me the final amount raised during the "sweep," I was floored: $12,000! The festivities included a car wash and sales of "We Believe #22" car stickers. Some local restaurants, like Kelley's Kafe, even donated proceeds from their sales that day. No one could possibly ask for more from their community. I felt really honored.

That's the spirit everyone in my life, and many people I didn't even know, was sharing with me in some manner practically every day during my recovery. Everybody was rooting for me. Word of my spinal cord injury spread rapidly, helped in part by stories popping up in the news media. *The Post-Intelligencer* in Seattle ran one article a couple of weeks after the accident at Central Washington University, and they wrote an update a few months later. KOMO-TV in Seattle covered my story in a segment soon after it happened, too. Brock Huard, who grew up in our area and later played quarterback for the Seahawks, did a feature on me for ESPN radio in Seattle. All those media accounts emphasized my positive attitude, as well as the enthusiastic support I had been receiving from my family and friends. This media coverage seemed to hit a positive nerve in the Spanaway-Puyallup area, and I was the beneficiary of hearty well-wishes from every corner.

I felt overwhelmed by this outpouring of caring at times, but I did my best to soak it all in. I knew that the challenges ahead of me remained steep, because being in the controlled environment of the hospital is very different from being turned back out into "real" life. As I discovered right away, it was going to be a life where so much was the same ... and yet so much was very, very different.

For starters, I was going back to live with Dad and Sally in our family home in Puyallup. The same, familiar place to eat and sleep, right? Hardly. We had a very nice house, but it was not built with the idea of having a teenage kid in a wheelchair living in it. While I was rehabbing at Good Sam, my dad and Grandpa were busy remodeling our house so it could accommodate my needs. They did a tremendous job! They ripped out a wall, tore up the carpet and put laminate in, and added a back door so I could get out of the house faster and more safely in an emergency. They converted what had once been Aaron's room, and then a family room after he moved out, into my bedroom.

They also had to remodel the bathroom adjacent to my bedroom to make it accessible. Grandpa's skills as an electrician were really put to use in that project! The new walk-in shower wasn't quite ready when I came home, so my first shower was performed under the same garden hose that used to serve as the goal line for our backyard football field. My dad told me later that he considered building a giant "S" on the shower wall (for Superman), although that plan remained on the drawing board. Sally also was right there adding her efforts, energy, and caring touch to the re-invention of the Seelye household. Others joined in, too. Jordyn's best friend Lindsey and her family took on the critical task of building a wheelchair ramp at our front entrance.

Of course, it wasn't just the physical configuration of the house that was going to be different. The changes would show up in everything I did, and all the ways that I needed my family to help me do them. While I had nurses assisting me in the shower at the hospital, my dad was the one to help me once we got our new shower operational. Using the catheter was also still part of my routine, and you can imagine the challenge that presented within a family environment. On those occasions that I had accidents in the middle of the night because of the difficulty of getting up, my dad was right there to deal with that situation. I did my best to demonstrate independence in other areas of day-to-day life, but the reality was that I was dependent on Dad and Sally a lot.

Even though I had obtained my learner's permit before the accident, I wasn't ready for driving. My dad was kind enough to buy me a Honda Accord that summer, but because it had a stick shift, I knew I wasn't going to be able to drive it. At Good Sam, I did spend some time working with one of the therapists who specializes in teaching patients how to drive. However, when he introduced me to hand controls, I just wasn't comfortable. So I let go of the idea of driving for a while.

As well as helping to attend to my basic needs, my dad also served as one of my primary cheerleaders. I remember all the ways he would urge me to strengthen my legs: encouraging me to stand for 30 minutes at a time, or urging me to try walking several steps on the street outside our home. "This time try walking for 100 feet without stopping to rest," he would say. He would also remind me to take my muscle relaxant medication every few hours, even waking me up to come downstairs to take the pill. These routines sure were different from those football-playing days when he introduced me to Creatine to build muscle mass and cooked me steak and eggs with potatoes to beef up my body. My needs had changed, and so had my goals.

What we went through together during those first months, and throughout my final two years of high school, opened the door for a great deal of bonding in my family. However, I've got to be honest here. We also hit upon our fair share of tension and conflict. My parents had divorced when I was 11, and my dad married Sally when I was 13. As often happens with teenagers with divorced parents, I really struggled to adjust to the new relationships and changed family dynamics. And that was *before* I came home with a spinal cord injury! So in those first two post-injury years, the sparks would sometimes fly, and words were occasionally spoken that really stung.

However, we weathered those storms and, over time, we were able to emerge with stronger relationships. My dad was a constant source of guidance, encouragement, and hands-on support, and Sally really stepped up with critical care-taking around the house. When I look back at that period today, one dominant feeling comes right to the surface: *gratitude*. I am very thankful for all the sacrifices made, and the devoted attention showered on me while we were all doing our best to handle the new roles and new ways within the same environment we had known.

I can now more deeply appreciate how hard my injury must have been for my dad. He could no longer look forward to sitting in the stands on Friday night during Sentinels' football games and watching his son, #22, continue to hunt down ball-carriers or smash into receivers. No more would he feel so invested in Spanaway Lake High games that he would be stirred to make comments like, "Ref, what are you, blind?" One of his sons had begun really making it in football, the game he always wanted to play but was forbidden to engage in, and the prospects for greater accomplishments had been looking very strong. With my injury he lost … not his son, but an important aspect of his son. Maybe, in some ways, he had begun to live through me during my rapid rise in the sport that I excelled in. But you know what? I loved every minute of it!

There was a time after I got out of Good Sam when my dad would even talk about how I was going to baffle all the doctors and defy the odds to play football again someday. He once set up a five-year plan for doing just that. I have to admit, I didn't really take the goal literally. Yes, I was absolutely determined to walk fully on my own one day, but I understood that rehabbing to the point of playing football was not going to be part of the picture. I accepted my dad's idea as a symbolic reminder of the need to set goals and work hard to achieve them, and eventually he was able to let go of the image of his son getting back on the playing field.

The void of not having football in my life was also intensely felt by another family member. My brother Adam really struggled with seeing his brother in a wheelchair, not able to get on with such a promising high school football career. Adam had graduated from Spanaway Lake High not long before my injury, and he soon moved far from home. There was a period there in which he and I became much more estranged, and it wasn't just because of the physical distance between us. Adam was devastated because of what was "taken away" from me. He also felt a strong sense of injustice.

"This should have happened to me, not Logan!" he would say. As Adam was quick to admit, he had fallen into a phase of smoking dope and acting out, which began even before he graduated from high school and continued after he moved out of our house. In contrast, he looked at me as the "perfect" one. It would be a long time before my brother and I found our way back to the closeness we once knew, and although I was disappointed to see him drift off, I also understood. What happened to me was definitely hard on Adam.

While I was figuring out how to navigate life at home, I also had to adjust to being a high school student in a wheelchair. On that first day of steering my wheelchair through the familiar corridors of our high school, I felt both nervous and embarrassed. How would all the other students react to seeing one of their former football players being unable to walk? Would they stare? Would they avoid me? Would they make comments that spilled over the edge, even for a kid who liked humor?

I guess I didn't need to worry. As it turned out, I was totally accepted just as I was, with all my needs, limitations, and dependencies. Things like going to see the nurse and using a catheter to use the boys' room soon became a matter of routine. My friend Steven still laughs about his "Logan Seelye Lunch Pass" that allowed him to buy two lunches in the cafeteria line: one for himself and one for me (mostly!). Also, I was still the same solid student I had been before the accident, and I still liked my favorite teachers.

If I wasn't using my wheelchair, I relied on leg braces for support. I never did like those braces. I just wasn't comfortable with being dependent on anything to help me move, I guess. I knew that the leg braces were there to help me, but that just reminded me that I *needed* help, which made me feel in some ways like I wasn't progressing. As much as I disliked braces, I was even more against using crutches. I just didn't feel stable with arm crutches. If you start to lose your balance, you might end up falling forward. At least with a walker, if you begin to lose your balance, you can just lean into the walker for support. It was just a matter of searching for my comfort zone, and there was a lot of searching to do as a high school student with a spinal cord injury.

It helped that those first days back in school also coincided with the start of the 2003 Spanaway Lake High football season.

Thanks to the attitude of complete acceptance that started with Coach Ro and ran through all the players, I was still considered very much part of the team. No, I wasn't going to be sniffing out pass patterns or charging to the line from my safety position to bust up a running play behind the line of scrimmage. Still, I was present for every practice, and every game.

Come Friday night, I still had a role to play. Coach Ro entrusted me with calling our defensive signals, which were relayed onto the field for our defense by one of the assistant coaches. While performing this important task, I would be wearing my neck brace while strategically positioned behind Justin Miller, an offensive lineman who probably weighed 300 pounds and who would protect me in case a player happened to go charging out of bounds in my vicinity. One of the assistant coaches even helped me use my catheter. Some people at the game would stare at me on the sidelines, but I didn't care. It just felt great to be wanted by the team.

"When the season began, we were all eager to get back out there again because we loved football," Steven recalls. "But in one way it didn't feel right—Logan was not out there with us. We wanted our leader! It helped to have him on the sidelines calling signals, but the moment I remember is when he called the team together before a game against Emerald Ridge. He gave a little speech, told us how he wished he could be playing with us, and then he took off his jacket to reveal brand new Spanaway Lake Sentinels team jerseys. Wow! We rushed back into the locker room, changed into those clean new jerseys, and stormed back onto the field for the game. That's when it felt like Logan was really with us!"

Steven still kids me about my defensive play-calling. When I called for a blitz on almost every third-down play, I would laugh and say, "I'm just playing Madden (video game)." After the game, one of the opposing team's coaches approached me and said, "You sure blitz a lot." I just smiled and shouted to myself, "Madden!"

My friend Brandon noticed right away that my teammates had taken the enthusiasm and unity they had surrounded me with every day in the corridors of Good Samaritan Hospital and transferred it into a mission to win football games. "As his friends and teammates, it was a situation where either you get torn apart by what happened or it draws you closer together," he explains. "We got closer."

It was fun for me to see my buddy Brandon taking over what would have been my spot as one of our two safeties.

"I knew how bad Logan wanted to be out there, so I thought to myself, 'What does Logan most want to see in me?' The answer was intensity," Brandon remembers. "So right from the first game, I was going to make that my mentality. Blindside comeback hits became my specialty, though they are illegal today. I won our team's Big Hitter of the Year award. It was the best football year of my life.

"I got to share one memorable moment with Logan. Our team had the ball, which meant that I was on the sidelines with our defense. I was talking seriously to Logan about something, I don't know what, when suddenly the other team got the ball back. I rushed out to take my safety position on defense. It was late in the game, and we had a slim lead, and I noticed that our opponent's top defensive back was now playing offense for the first time. 'Oh, they're going to throw it to him,' I said to myself. Sure enough, I read the play correctly and intercepted the pass. As I rushed back to the sidelines, I went right back to where I had been standing next to Logan and said, 'Now, as I was saying.' The memory still cracks both of us up."

I wasn't laughing the night Ro called me to come out on the field during halftime of another Spanaway Lake High game. The team and the whole community of Spanaway had recently held another fundraising event for me, this time an auction. NFL quarterback and local hero Jon Kitna had donated a signed Cincinnati Bengals jersey and Lawyer Milloy, another former player from our area who went on to a long, successful NFL career, had contributed a signed football or some other valuable and personal item. Ro handed me the microphone, and I was more nervous than I had ever been before a big play on the field. I mean, how do you thank all these people you knew and those you didn't know for being so kind, generous, and supportive? I struggled to find the right words, but once again everyone accepted me, just the way I was.

So my teammates gave me a taste of the familiar, which went a long way to help ease the emptiness of not playing football. When the team wasn't practicing or playing games, they still invited me to hang out with them. I remember the day we were clowning around at my house when I fell and accidentally landed in Brandon's lap.

"Dude, why are you in my lap?" he said with a serious expression.

"I just fell over," I explained, and in response he threw me on my bed, prompting us all to burst out laughing ... just as we would laugh in the old days.

Something else special happened during my senior season with the Sentinels. We didn't play our home games at our school because the bleachers only held 60 or 70 people, and we had a lot more fans than that. So only our junior varsity team played at Spanaway Lake, while the varsity shared a playing facility with Bethel High School about 10 minutes away. During my senior year, the new Art Crate Stadium at that site was unveiled during our first home game against Puyallup High, and I was chosen to lead the ribbon-cutting ceremony. I summoned the strength to walk the entire way to midfield, with my walker, while Ro carried the game ball. The crowd roared at the sight of me moving on my own. In a way, that moment was just as big a thrill as intercepting a pass to save a game!

During all this time of adjusting to being a student at Spanaway Lake and keeping up with my teammates in the ways that I still could, I was also maintaining my rehab treatment as an out-patient at Good Sam. You can bet that Donna and Corrine and the rest of the staff were not taking it any easier on me, just because I had a full day-to-day school and home schedule to keep up! I would report for rehab for two hours before school every morning, and I can vividly recall those mornings when Corrine would get me working so hard trying to walk that I would have to dump water all over my head when we were done. When I got to school, I would have to ask a classmate to get me a dry T-shirt.

A few months after the injury, my dad took me to Seattle to see the neurosurgeon who performed my surgery. I had another check-up with him about a year post-surgery, so he could evaluate my progress and examine how well my fifth and sixth vertebrae were meshing together. I don't know if he remembered telling me after the surgery that I would never have feeling or movement below chest level, but he certainly took note of the surprising degree of sensation and function I had regained. He seemed genuinely excited to see my progress. I also think he understood that it was nothing that I didn't expect of myself. I always knew I was going to improve. I was determined to live my life to the fullest, whatever that meant, and I wasn't going to give up on my goals—including walking totally on my own some day.

My positive attitude was fueled by the continued enthusiastic support of my family, my football teammates, and the entire Spanaway community. On top of all that was the special support of Jordyn, not only my girlfriend but my biggest rooter and best friend. That was one part of life that had not changed: Jordyn was still right there in the center of that life! Our love remained constant and unshaken. Some people might have been surprised that a couple who began dating in junior high school not only could survive all the crazy changes you go through during adolescence but also the huge challenges brought on by my spinal cord injury. We weren't surprised, though. We knew.

To explain how Jordyn and I got together, I have to go all the way back to seventh grade. At that time, Jordyn's sister Kimiko had a crush on me. Miko was in my class, with Jordyn a year older. When Miko would go home and tell her older sister about this boy named Logan who was "so cute, so athletic, and so smart," Jordyn was not initially impressed. I wasn't really drawn to ask Miko out, so she started dating my buddy Andy Griffin. Andy and I were like brothers back then, and at one point Andy approached me with an idea: "Wouldn't it be cool if we brothers double-dated the sisters?!" That meant Jordyn and I would wind up together. I agreed to this plan because I thought Jordyn was cute and athletic, and the sisters signed on to it too. We all wound up going to a movie together, but in no way do Jordyn and I consider that our "first date." She thought I was a punk, which, I must admit, I kind of was in those days. I was something of a bully and just a real jackass in seventh and eighth grade, the time when my parents were going through their divorce.

So Jordyn found a "real" boyfriend, and I had a girlfriend, but our paths never veered far apart. Jordyn was a serious volleyball player and also played softball, which meant we hung around the same group of athlete friends. Soon we began talking more, and when her boyfriend broke up with her, during a basketball game at school, I was the one who consoled her. Before long we were talking on the phone at night, and soon it was every night, sometimes for as long as three hours! We also noticed this little coincidence related to our contact: Whenever something important was happening, or being talked about, the time always seemed to be exactly 9:33. We began to eagerly anticipate the next 9:33 moment.

Strangely, I was still dating my girlfriend, Darcy, who attended another school, while Jordyn and I were both still at Cedarcrest Junior High. During our long phone calls, Jordyn and I would debate the pros and cons of "Logan being with Darcy" vs. "Logan being with Jordyn." After a full and *totally* impartial discussion with Jordyn and her sister Miko, "Logan being with Jordyn" won.

"I knew he wanted to ask me out," Jordyn recalls. "But I told him, 'You can't do it in a note; you can't do it on the phone; you have to do it in person.' He was always chicken about things like that."

One night after a basketball game, Jordyn's mom Susie took us all out to Dairy Queen. We were having a good time when suddenly Susie turned to Jordyn and asked her to go to her car to get some creamer for her coffee. While Jordyn was heading to the car, Susie turned to me.

"Logan, you should go out with Jordyn," she said.

"What? You mean out to the car?" I asked. "Or do you mean really *go out*?"

Susie didn't have to answer. I followed her advice and rushed to catch up with Jordyn. She turned to look behind her as she entered the car, and there I was. I managed to speak the words I needed to say, in a nervous, high-pitched voice, and Jordyn immediately said "yes." We noted the time: It was exactly 9:33 p.m.! And the date was 3/9. The signs were all in alignment.

I immediately broke up with Darcy, though I had to do it through a friend because I lacked the nerve to tell her myself. The funny thing is, Jordyn and I didn't actually go out on a date anytime soon after that March 9, 2001, pronouncement. We just became boyfriend and girlfriend. Our "dating" was mostly just hanging out at Jordyn's house, a beautiful home in the country with a fantastic view of Mount Rainier. I always felt comfortable there because Susie truly treated me as one of the family. Jordyn and I just had fun with whatever we happened to be doing, even if that meant letting Jordyn and Miko dress Andy and me up in girls' clothes, complete with makeup and jewelry! We finally did go out, just to see some movie whose title neither of us remembers and dinner at TGI Fridays, which we chose because we could walk to get there and didn't need to be driven by an adult.

People could see that we just fit together as a couple. When we were both in high school, Coach Ro told me, "I'm really big on young men respecting women, and I could tell right away that you respected Jordyn. Your relationship was very impressive, not just the public displays of affection but just the way you were around each other. My heart took a lot of pictures of what I was seeing."

That first year we were dating was my eighth grade and Jordyn's ninth grade, and the following year she began high school while I was still at Cedarcrest. That meant that we didn't see each other during the day, and I was spending more and more time with my buddies from the football and basketball teams. One day Jordyn confronted me about this.

"Do you just want to hang out with the guys, or do you want to be with me?" she asked. "If it's the guys, we're going to need to break up."

She told me this over the phone when I was hanging out at my buddy Derek's house. When I hung up, I rushed out of his house and started to run the 10 miles from Spanaway to her house in Graham as fast as I could.

"Don't break up with me!" I pleaded when I arrived, panting, at Jordyn's door. I even started crying at the thought of us breaking up, and I vowed to change how I was acting and put her first in our relationship.

She didn't break up with me, of course, and when I got to high school, in that sophomore year when football became so important, we had some of our best times. We kept up a tradition of celebrating the 9th of every month, since we officially began "dating" on March 9th. We would make our own cards, with our own drawings, to give to each other on that day. Jordyn told me that I used "sweeter" words in my cards than the rest of our time together. I suppose she was right.

The cards kept coming after the accident, though my drawings got a little sketchier because of the limited use of my hands. In almost everything we did, we just kept on the way we had been going before my injury. Jordyn still wore my football jersey at home games, and I got to root her on during her volleyball games. The Spanaway Lake High girls' volleyball team rose to a #3 ranking in the state of Washington!

Jordyn would have driven me to school after my morning rehab workouts at Good Sam, since I didn't like riding the bus for "handicapped" students, but she had volleyball practice early in the morning. Her sister Miko stepped in. One day, while I was alone in my house before Miko arrived, I fell and couldn't get off the floor. Somehow Miko figured out what was going on and climbed in through the window to get me. We both got a kick out of telling Jordyn about that one.

So with Jordyn at my side, and so many other people standing with me, it was easy for me to keep believing, to keep my spirits up, to focus on the truth that life really is only 10 percent what happens to you and 90 percent how you react to it. I remember an assignment for Spanish class in which we were asked to choose a favorite saying and translate it from English to

Spanish. I chose that inspirational 10-and-90 quote, which Coach Ro had first shared with me in my hospital bed in Seattle during those first days after the accident.

"Life is 10 percent what happens to you, and 90 percent how you react to it."

People around me noticed that I was living by this positive attitude. I could really feel it at our high school graduation. It was already a great day, anyway, because I had learned that I would be graduating 22nd in our class. There was that number again, 22, my uniform number when I played football for the Spanaway Lake Sentinels. When they called my name during the graduation ceremony, I confidently wheeled up on to the stage, stood up and, with the aid of a walker, I walked across the stage and accepted my diploma. At that moment, the entire crowd of students, teachers, and families stood and cheered.

I believed, and they believed with me. It was an amazing moment!

CHAPTER SIX

The Road to Independence

I ALWAYS KNEW THAT I would be going to college, and suffering a spinal cord injury was not going to hold me back. I had seen other teenagers from our area who decided not to go on to college, or who chose to take a year off before continuing their education—which, as it turned out, never happened. Most of these kids just drifted from job to job and hung out around town, with no real ambition. That wasn't me. I may have had physical limitations, but I was still firmly committed to creating a satisfying future, both personally and professionally.

During my junior year of high school, however, the image I had in mind was of attending Pierce Community College close to home. That image, I have to admit, emerged from feeling at least somewhat limited. I figured I could take a bus to my classes while still living with my dad and Sally in Puyallup. It would be convenient and easy. I would earn my Associates Degree and then see what might come after that. It seemed to make sense.

Then I got to thinking about it some more. It didn't take me long to realize that I did not want to live my life with "convenient and easy" as my rallying cry. I also knew it was time to leave home after graduating from high school, and I would just have to figure out how to manage doing so. As difficult as it might be to live on my own, to learn how to fully take care of myself, I needed to go away to college. And I knew just the college that would be right for me.

The decision was solidified during the summer after my junior year at Spanaway Lake High School. I took a trip with the football team that landed on the grounds of a college. I loved the campus, liked the feel of the nearby town, and felt aligned with the academic offerings. Yes, this was just the college for me: Central Washington University!

That's right: I was going back to the scene of the football collision that landed me in a wheelchair. Some people might think that the location in which I suffered the injury that derailed my football dreams and dramatically changed my life would be the last place I would want to spend the next four years of my life. Those people would be wrong. In making my important choices in the spirit that life is only 10 percent what happens to you and 90 percent how you react to it, I was not thinking about what to avoid. I was thinking about what I would take on, with all my heart.

Ironically, it was that summer trip with the Spanaway Lake High football team that helped make up my mind. There I was, attending the same Central Washington University summer camp I had participated in a year earlier, when I was capturing the attention of opposing players and coaches with my quick reads from my safety position and my jarring tackles on running backs and wide receivers. Being on that same football field where I hit that Redmond High receiver and did not get up from the collision certainly stirred my emotions. I shed a tear or two, but I didn't linger there. I was on a new mission: to check out the campus while envisioning getting around on my own—without my father, without Jordyn, without all my primary support team. Could I really manage the task of transporting myself from dorm to classrooms to dining hall to library to wherever I needed or wanted to go to enjoy the full college experience? Was I really ready for *that* kind of independence?

I took my time maneuvering around campus, making mental notes about hills, curves, rough terrain. I was trying to imagine what could cause problems for a guy in a wheelchair. It didn't seem so bad. I believed that I could handle it. I would find a way to meet whatever challenges might come along. Of course, it helped that I liked the campus so much and really loved Ellensburg. The town had such a calm, quiet nature. The weather was beautiful, although I knew it could get windy and I had heard that snow, which was a rarity back home in Puyallup and Spanaway, could really pile on sometimes in the winter. I guess I just decided that I would figure that out when the time came, too.

I never even applied to any other college. I have to admit, I didn't study for my SATs, and my scores stunk. Fortunately, that did not prevent me from being accepted, although it did mean that I would be taking remedial math and English as a freshman. That thought did not discourage me, either. I was going away to college!

I didn't have any concrete career goal in mind, or any sense of what I really wanted to study. I was just excited to live on my own and ready to have some fun, to let loose some of the frustration of living with my injury and allow myself to be a "normal" college guy.

I don't remember my dad sitting down with me to share any concerns or anxiety about the idea of me going off on my own. By the time I graduated from high school, I was already doing more and more for myself. Our household had its share of tension that comes with having any strong-willed teenager in the house. We were all ready for a change.

My dad was right on board with me when he drove me the two hours from Puyallup to Ellensburg for Freshman Orientation, a week or two before classes were to begin. In the midst of listening to the overview of what to expect when living on campus, how to study, and how to locate important places, I met an incoming freshman who was getting around in a motorized wheelchair. When we talked, I learned that he had a muscular dystrophy disease that caused his muscles to weaken very quickly and severely limited his mobility. He introduced me to his "friend," a black lab on a leash attached to his wheelchair that would go with him wherever he went, even jumping up to push the blue handicap buttons to automatically open doors for him. It felt reassuring to meet someone else who would be navigating the challenges of getting around campus in a wheelchair, although I was fully committed to keeping my hand-powered wheelchair because I still didn't feel comfortable relying on a motorized version.

Despite a basic sense of confidence, I was still nervous when my dad and I drove back to Ellensburg for move-in day. I guess many freshmen feel those butterflies about all the newness about to come pouring into their lives. Like everyone around me, I would have to make new friends, adjust to new hours, make more decisions on my own, and establish an identity for myself in a totally different environment from high school. Then there was the added factor of living with a spinal cord injury.

I was carrying one of my bags on my lap while wheeling up to one of the check-in tents when I spotted a familiar face: Jacob Skordal. Jacob and I had been going to school together since seventh grade and were football teammates both at Cedarcrest Junior High and at Spanaway Lake High.

"Dude!" we each yelled at the other. I had heard that Jacob had also enrolled at Central Washington, but I didn't know until we got to talking under that arrival tent that we were going to be living in the same dorm. I would be on the first floor, and he would be living right above me on the second floor. That piece of news gave me an instant sense of relief. My good friend Brandon also was attending Central Washington as a sophomore. I was not going to be totally alone.

After check-in procedures were completed, I was eager to see my dorm room. I had called the school when dorm assignments were being made to ask about how I would be able to get around in my room. I still carried images from staying in the Central Washington University dorms during my first summer football camp in 2003, when we had been assigned to small, cramped rooms. When I tried to imagine what it would be like to share that space with a roommate, I was filled with questions: How would I maneuver around in my wheelchair? How would I take a shower in that tiny shower stall? Or would I have to use a communal bathroom? "Don't worry, we'll take care of that," they told me.

Still, the same questions bubbled up again as I approached my dorm room. When I opened the door, however, the questions vanished. My room was huge ... and it was all mine! It must have been the size of two of those other dorm rooms I had stayed in put together. It was fully handicapped accessible, with my own bathroom complete with a large shower and sink. The people in charge of dorm assignments really had taken care of me! After a final orientation with my RA (resident advisor), it was time to say goodbye to my dad and begin life on my own.

I never asked about any "special needs" considerations regarding transportation around campus. I really liked my private, accessible room, but it happened to be located on the north end of campus. My classes, unfortunately, were either in mid-campus or on the far southern end. That was no problem going to class because it was mostly downhill, but when class was over I had to wheel back uphill. I would often cramp up from fatigue, but I just kept going. I was too proud to ask for help.

Rainy days were the hardest. My hands would get very wet, not only from the rain but also from grabbing the wheels when they began to get wet as well. Pushing myself along in the slippery conditions was difficult, even for a former football player like me, because of limited strength in my hands. I even tried wearing a pair of my old football gloves to see if the sticky grip on them would help, but once they got wet it was still really slippery, causing it to be hard to maneuver in certain situations. One evening it was raining so hard when I got out of class that I knew it would be really hard for me to try to go back to my room without help, and even if I did manage to make it back, I would be soaking wet. "Jake, I have a weird request," I said when I texted my friend Jacob. "Can you come down to the University Center and take me back up to our dorm?" I felt embarrassed that I couldn't do something on my own, and I felt even worse that Jacob had to come all the way out from our dorm to where I was and then push me all the way back. As it turned out, Jacob didn't mind at all, and he did it without complaint. Another challenge had been met.

Of course, when the snow arrived a few months into the school year, I had to face an even tougher obstacle. The snow would pile up on the wheels of my wheelchair and get all over me. When I would finally find my way to my classroom, my pants and the sides of my shirt would be soaked, and my hands, beyond being cold and dirty, were caked in the salt that the campus grounds crew had laid down to help prevent students from slipping while walking. Small rocks and ice had also been churning up on my wrists. Before I sat down in class, I would go to the men's room to grab paper towels to at least partially dry myself off. When class was over, it was time for the uphill climb in the snow. Fortunately, some of the snow and ice on the walkways would be melted from the heated water channeled down through pipes from above, but I wasn't so lucky as this pathway was not part of my journey back to the dorms unless I wanted to spend another 10 minutes taking the "scenic" route. Then I also had to deal with major cross-over intersections where I had to navigate two lanes of traffic. The cars driving back and forth over the snow would push up snow and slush that would form a wall of debris that I could not get through. When I ran into that roadblock, I would have to detour more than 100 feet along one sidewalk to get back to my route to the dorm. I have to admit that I asked for help more than once in these snowy conditions, and sometimes the person I reached out to was someone I hardly knew. Matter of fact, I can remember one time very explicitly. I was trying to cross the road and, sure enough, I got stuck in the wall of snow in the middle of the road. I was trying to push through it, but I kept on spinning out and basically got stuck. Luckily, some guy was kind enough to get out of his car and help push me through it and up onto the sidewalk. It wasn't exactly ideal circumstances to make a new friend!

At least I no longer had to seek assistance for an everyday need that had become more frustrating and embarrassing over the months after my spinal cord injury. I'm talking about going to the bathroom. While I had learned to accept help in using the catheter, it would still sometimes make me feel weak or useless. I was reminded of how I had always been such an independent person before the injury, and having someone with me while doing something so personal was one of the most difficult offshoots of having a spinal cord injury. Add in the fact that I had begun to have feelings *everywhere* in my body and this had become an even more uncomfortable situation. Before I moved into my room at Central Washington, I would often find myself wondering, *Will I have to find a nurse's office somewhere on campus every time I need to pee? What if no one can help me?*

Finally, I just began trying to relieve myself without the use of the catheter at all. By the time classes had begun, I was essentially free of the catheter. I can't tell you how liberating it felt just to be able to go into the bathroom, do my business, and leave. I still had to make special arrangements while I slept at night, but I could live with that. I was just thrilled to be free of asking for help in such a critical realm of life. It definitely helped me feel "normal" again. Around the same time I was also in the process of experiencing life without leg braces. Before I left home that summer, I was down to using a brace only on my right leg that extended from the knee down, and during my freshman year at college I shed that last brace! I would watch TV for 30 minutes at a time while standing with my walker, and then try to stand briefly without the walker.

I guess you could say I was a normal college freshman in many ways. First, I would get nervous about some of the new circumstances in my life. Every first-year college student wants to be accepted, and for me that was complicated by my injury. The other students didn't act so differently toward me most of the time, but many of them would stare at me in my wheelchair. I remember one male student in a Creative Writing class who just wouldn't stop staring. I usually accepted the stares, assuming people were just being curious, but sometimes I would be bothered enough to make eye contact with the person staring to make them look away. Well, that didn't work with this guy. We sat in groups of five or six students at tables, and he just sat there in my table with his constant stare. Sometimes, he would scan his eyes up and down my wheelchair. Finally, one day I had had enough.

"Dude, why are you staring? What's your deal?" I asked.

"Oh, uh, I'm just confused," he said. "Why are you in the wheelchair?"

Once again, it was just someone's curiosity. I was fine with telling him what had happened to me, but I still wondered if he understood how rude it was to keep staring like that. If he wanted to ask me about it, why couldn't he have just asked? Fortunately, most of the students weren't like that. More often than not, once they took the time to get to know me, they realized I was just a regular guy. I can remember hanging out watching sports on ESPN with Jacob and some of his buddies in the dorm one night when one of those awkward moments came up. I started talking to them about football, and they looked at me a bit strangely, as if to say, "Dude, you're in a wheelchair, what do you know about football?"I didn't rush in to tell them about my sophomore year on the Spanaway Lake High varsity football team, or how I was tearing up the summer football camp there at Central Washington before I got injured. But when I showed them that I knew all about the Seahawks' current battle for starting positions, they began treating me the same as anybody else.

For me, getting used to new circumstances extended way beyond the social scene. I was still busy getting used to new things like taking a shower on my own. Even in my accessible dorm room, I would get a little antsy when I went to use the shower because I was still not 100 percent confident of performing that task on my own.

Then there was the matter of my eating habits. I was well acquainted with the term "freshman 15," a reference to how many pounds freshmen often gain during their first year of college. I learned the truth of this expression the hard way. I had always been in excellent physical shape, of course, only gaining weight during a period in which I was also adding strength and endurance while training for football. Even after the injury, I never really gained much weight, although I did lose some of that hard-earned muscle mass. Now, with a meal plan that enabled me to have meals at a small dining area/grocery store not far from my dorm, I found myself following a regular diet of pizza, hamburgers, french fries, milk shakes, baked potatoes, donuts, and similar fare. While I may not have reached the "freshman 15" level in the first couple of months, I sure did notice some extra rolls here and there.

I also got used to being more normal about the act of getting my own food. Remember, my friends would fill my tray and bring it to me in high school. I knew that wasn't going to happen here in college. I soon discovered that the act of putting my own food on a tray in my lap was a breeze most of the time. Occasionally, I might need a hand, but since that wasn't often I had no problem asking a buddy or even a student I didn't know.

Another area in which I could call myself a normal freshman was going through an adjustment to the academic side of college life. Let's just say those days of ranking near the top of my high school class were far off in the rear-view mirror! Before I reveal my first-semester GPA, I need to point out that the remedial math and English classes that I was required to take because of my poor SAT scores did not even count toward my GPA. That left just two classes, one of which I earned an A in. The other class, Economics, was something I just couldn't grasp, as evidenced by a D for my final grade. This was quite a wake-up call for a guy who never received anything less than an A-minus in high school. Worse, it knocked my GPA down to a 1.5. At that time, anyone who finished with a GPA under 2.0 as a freshman had to take an academic probation class and get lectured about the importance of studying and working hard in school.

If you had asked me then whether I needed such redirection, I probably would have laughed. However, as I look back at that freshman adjustment period today, well, I guess I didn't take my classes *totally* seriously as my college career was getting off the ground. Let's just say I was amazed to discover that a student could actually choose to remain in his dorm room, just relaxing and playing video games, while one of his classes was going on. What an eye-opening experience! Oh, and there may have been occasions where I even allowed myself to do some drinking with the guys. Like I said, it seemed important to let loose and have some fun.

Fortunately, I had the good sense to get back to my more accustomed study habits before long. By my second semester, my grades had already improved, and those other choices that come with independence were falling at least a *little* more into alignment with the person I had known myself to be. I was still enjoying a great deal about college life and spending a lot of time with Brandon. However, there was one thing I had grown very accustomed to in my life back home that I badly missed.

Jordyn was not there.

I had missed her already during my senior year of high school. After graduating a year ahead of me, she had considered following up on feelers to play volleyball and attend a Division III college far from home. Instead, she had chosen to stay close by and enrolled at Green River College, a two-year school near Tacoma. She was still living with her mom and step-dad, so I could see her often, but I did miss being close to her every day in school. When I went away to Central Washington University, however, we hardly got together at all. That was a difficult change for both of us.

"I would worry about Logan being on his own. I would think, what if he falls down in the shower and no one knows about it?" Jordyn recalls. "Then he told me he was drinking. Wow, to me the body is a temple. I remember my volleyball coach telling us we couldn't drink or do drugs or it would mess us up. After a while, I came to accept that Logan just needed that time to be carefree, after everything that had happened to him, but I would still worry about him being with friends who were drinking. Maybe he would wind up in a car with a drunk driver."

That freshman year, we only saw each other three or four times. We still talked on the phone every night, but the stress from being apart was mounting. By summer, we knew it was time for a serious talk about our future. We had reached another choice point and had to decide what was really important. Once again, we landed on the same page: Jordyn was going to join me by enrolling at Central Washington herself. She found a program that perfectly fit her future goals in teaching, special education, and we found an apartment to live in together. We were taking another huge step in our relationship, and we were both totally behind the move. Like I said before, we were, and are, soul mates.

Moving in with Jordyn was a positive change in almost every facet of my life. She was able to drive me to my classes so I didn't have to deal with the steep uphill climb or slippery sidewalks. She helped me when it was time to go to the store and buy groceries. We were even able to take a film class and a religious studies class together. Part of enjoying an everyday life together was getting a dog. Jordyn had wanted a dog more than I did at the time, so the compromise was that I would agree to bring in a dog as long as I got to name it. When she picked out a cute little purse dog, I immediately named him Duce. I chose that name because my number had always been 22, or "deuce, deuce," which we shortened to just Duce. We enjoyed our first Thanksgiving together, on our own, during autumn in my sophomore year. Jordyn and I worked together, side by side, to prepare the turkey and all the fixings: potatoes, stuffing, green bean casserole, pumpkin pie. It was just one more way to totally enjoy one another's company and experience our love continuing to grow.

With Jordyn around, I became even more serious as a student. I still played video games and would go out to drink with the guys now and then, but my main focus, other than enjoying being with Jordyn, was now my school work. My grades continued to improve and, by the end of my sophomore year, I had zeroed in on a major. I remember one of my professors asking me what field I wanted to study and, when I couldn't answer him, he recommended that I pay a visit to my academic advisor. During our meeting, she asked me, "Do you like business?" and then, "Do you like technology?" When I immediately answered yes to both questions, she offered me a suggestion that wound up propelling me into my current career.

"Since you like business and technology, I recommend you study Information Technology and Administrative Management," she said.

That sounded good to me. In my junior year, I took an intro to web design class and was instantly hooked. My professor, Chuck Wahle, made learning about web design easy and fun, and I was eager to learn more. I claimed a specialization of "Web Design and Database Design" and moved toward my degree with that emphasis solidly in place. I boosted my graduating GPA up to a 3.2.

So I had a career goal, I lived in an apartment in a community I had come to love, and I had my girlfriend with me every day. I had weathered that adjustment to being a "normal" freshman, celebrated my independence and freedom, and steered my life in exciting new directions. *Life is 10 percent what happens to me and 90 percent how I react to it.* The 90 percent was shaping up more and more in a positive way.

Something else had changed. When Jordyn and I moved into our apartment, I had noticed a small workout area in the laundry building. Since I had completed my rehab at Good Samaritan Hospital back home, I really had not exercised in any kind of gym or fitness center. This workout room didn't have much: an all-in-one machine, where I did bench presses and curls, and a stationary bike, which I would ride for 10 or 15 minutes. Still, that was something, and when my friend Brandon found out about that workout area he was quick to get in my ear about getting my butt in there. There was no way I could say no to one of my old workout buddies from the Spanaway Lake High football team!

My college years began rushing by me, the way they do for most college kids, I suppose. Before I knew it, graduation was approaching. And with that date came a challenge that I accepted: I decided to enter the selection process for delivering the commencement address for the Central Washington University Class of 2009.

I wound up competing against 10 other candidates. It was sort of like being in the playoffs in football. In the interview, they asked what I would talk about. I made it clear that I would explain what had happened to me back in 2003, and how I had chosen to live my life since my dream was taken away. I had to craft the speech and practice it in front of the selection committee. I guess they must have thought that it worked well, because when it came time to select the graduate to give the key speech to 5,000-plus students, faculty, administrators, and families, they chose me!

I was deeply honored, and more than a little nervous. When I was introduced to provide the Commencement that day, it was a moment I will never forget. Here is the speech that I delivered:

Welcome to Central Washington University's 2009 Eastside graduation ceremony. My name is Logan Seelye, and I will be your commencement speaker for this long-awaited day! But before I begin, I just want to say congratulations to all of you here today: the students, your families, and the professors; our self-discipline and commitment has finally paid off.

During my time at CWU, I have experienced a roller-coaster of highs and lows—good times and challenging times. I am sure all of you can relate. These experiences are just one chapter of our incredible book of life. But most of all, the past four years have been a blast as I have made many new friends, making my "chapter" blessed with learning experiences and lifetime memories. I have had professors who truly are passionate about teaching and making a difference in our lives. These professors not only made the classroom an exciting venue to challenge us to ask why, but they also integrated projects and ideas that apply to the "real" world. Let me share with you one of my most profound educational experiences here at Central.

My junior year, I was required to take a leadership class. Going into that class, I was thinking to myself: Man, is this going to be another boring class that might put me to sleep? But I was in for an incredible surprise. We were asked to choose a leadership book to read followed later by an in-depth report. For some of us, like me, this is not our favorite task. However, this book put things in place, making sense out of my educational opportunity at Central. I was wrong about this class and this report.

The book, "The 21 Indispensible Qualities of a Leader" by Dr. John C. Maxwell, explains the qualities found in leaders and how the qualities transcend into followers. Although all the qualities presented by Maxwell are powerful, the two that were most prominent during my studies and life in general are: 1) self-discipline; and 2) commitment.

Let me preface my perspective on these two qualities with my personal story. As you all can see, I am in a wheelchair, but I have not always been in this chair. Six years ago, on July 2nd, 2003, here at Central Washington—actually on these same fields, right behind you—something happened that unexpectedly changed my life forever. I was participating in the annual Central-sponsored football camp, with my high school football team. On the last day of camp during the second of three scheduled scrimmages, I made an amazing play on the field. I tackled the opposing team's wide receiver, forcing him to lose the ball and resulting in one of my teammates intercepting it and running it back for a touchdown. However, this is where my story of leadership begins.

While my coaches and teammates were cheering my feat, I lay on the ground motionless; I broke my neck and suffered a spinal cord injury. I was scared. I was awake and conscious, but it felt like my entire body was on fire. I was immediately taken to the hospital, given a steroid shot in my spine to slow down the swelling, and then airlifted to Harborview Hospital in Seattle for immediate neck surgery. A week later, as I lay in the hospital bed, slowly regaining the strength in only my shoulders, I thought to myself, "I can either complain and ask, why me, why did this happen? Or I can fight this situation and beat it." It was at this very moment when I was beginning to ponder self-discipline and commitment. As I was talking with one of the doctors, I asked him where my life would be going. With a bold face he looked at me and said, "You will never be able to walk again or have feeling/movement from your nipples down." As he walked away, I was thinking to myself, "This guy must be crazy to think I believe that!" And from that point forward, I have been committed to the self-discipline to prove him wrong.

These two concepts, self-discipline and commitment, have played such an important role in my life, as I believe they are important for all of us, not just leaders. I know many of you understand my story as you too have found yourself, in various degrees, exercising self-discipline and commitment. Nowadays, due to my rigorous and painstaking commitment and discipline, I am able to walk with a walker, drive a car, and work out five times a week. Yes, I live a normal life. But it is because I committed myself to doing so, to walking again, just as you all have been committed and self-disciplined to graduate from CWU. And guess what, you all did it. That is why you are sitting here and celebrating with me today.

Graduating from college is not a simple task for many of us. It takes a lot of commitment and self-discipline. But just like my leadership class, and the book report, I knew I would get the job done. Like so many of my professors, they knew I—we—would get the job done through self-discipline and commitment.

We have all come far in the past four or more years, not because we were lucky, not because we took the "easy way out," but because we worked hard and committed ourselves to doing something great: graduating from CWU. So let's celebrate! Be proud of yourself; be proud of what you have accomplished, but most of all, be proud of the leader that you have all become while studying here at Central. You and I have earned this honor! Congratulations to the Graduating Class of 2009 at Central Washington University.

I was amazed by how many people came up to me after the graduation ceremony. It was almost overwhelming to receive all the congratulations for graduating, but on top of that all the compliments for my speech.

"I was sitting there just wanting him to do a great job with the speech, but what he delivered was totally amazing to me," remembers Coach Ro. "There were many moments when my feelings were so strong, I just had to walk away to collect myself."

That was the first time I had the experience of simply telling my story and witnessing the dramatic impact it could have on other people. Perhaps I had a gift to offer, and I could find opportunities to extend that gift to many others.

CHAPTER SEVEN

The Gift of a Soul Mate

THERE WAS NEVER REALLY ANY question about whether Jordyn and I would get married. The only question was: When?

"So when are you two going to get married?" our family and friends kept asking while we were living together at Central Washington University.

"Can you let us get through college first?" we would respond with a smile.

Some people, at least those who didn't know us well, might have wondered whether my spinal cord injury had in any way dragged down our relationship. After all, we started dating in junior high school when we were both athletes, full of physical strength and vitality. The sky was no limit to what we could do individually and together. Then I lost a significant degree of movement in my body from my chest down, and instead of reaching for the stars through my football career, I was mostly confined to a wheelchair, sweating and fighting to take even the smallest steps on my own. As a teenager and young adult, I had become dependent on my girlfriend for dozens of tasks I used to handle on my own without a thought or concern. Certainly that was going to create a major strain on our relationship, right? I mean, it was one thing to grit our teeth together and battle through those first rugged months of recovery and rehabilitation when I was 16, but we weren't kids anymore. We were college graduates, facing the long-term questions of family and children, jobs and career, and day-to-day quality of life. How could we possibly still stay vibrant and strong as a couple, marching fully forward on the same path?

What those doubters do not realize is that Jordyn and I were both living by the 10 and 90 spirit. It didn't matter what happened to either of us, as individuals or as a couple. It was how we reacted to it. And together, we continued to respond to my spinal cord injury with optimism and determination, along with love and trust. I honestly believe that when we were making the commitment to get married, our relationship was (and still is) as strong as it was not *in spite of* my injury but, in some ways, *because* of my injury. Yes, our relationship was amazing and wonderful before I got hurt, but it went soaring to new heights after it happened.

How? We had to learn how to love each other in completely new ways. No longer were we able to spend most of our time playing sports and watching each other play sports. No longer could we wrestle around with each other. No longer could I pick her up and carry her in my arms. Things that we once enjoyed and that as teenagers we had taken very much for granted had been taken away. There would be no getting around that reality. Yet, all these changes just opened my eyes to the other amazing parts about this woman I loved.

First on that list was her unwavering positive attitude toward my injury. She never once let me see her cry or show her fears or concerns. I know that she did cry and of course she had moments when she was worried about me. That was simply being with the reality of what life had dealt us. But the fact that she was able to show such strength and support when standing beside me made me realize how lucky I really was to have her in my life. Once, when I was being interviewed for a local newspaper story, Jordyn told the reporter that it didn't matter how long I had to use a wheelchair. She would still be by my side and even push me around in that wheelchair, if need be, until the day we die. I don't know about you, but to receive such kindness and deep love from the person closest to you brings out a feeling that no words could possibly describe. To have that commitment at such a young age, at a time in my life when my world had changed so drastically, meant everything to me. My belief that I had found my soul mate never wavered.

Not *everything* had been taken away from us. We could still talk together, laugh together, share simple moments together. We could still go out to a movie or dinner together. We could still touch, still show our affection and our natural desire for each other.

This leads us to the question that many people have probably wondered about with Jordyn and me but were afraid to ask: What about sex? It's actually kind of funny, but even today, many years into our marriage and now going around our community as parents of our 3-year-old daughter, Skylar, I sometimes get "the look." Some people may be seeing me as a stereotype, assuming that just because I use a wheelchair I can't walk, I can't be married to a beautiful woman, and I can't have a beautiful child of my own. I'm not angry when I see that look. It actually makes me want to chuckle. I know they're just being curious.

So, to answer the question, I can begin by acknowledging that as teenagers Jordyn and I were practicing safe sex before I got hurt. After the hit that derailed my football career, in addition to all the major life questions and huge unknowns ahead of me, I naturally found time to wonder about whether or not I'd still be able to be physically intimate with my girlfriend. Within a couple of weeks of my surgery at Harborview Hospital in Seattle, I had, shall we say, some positive signals. Of course I was quick to share this good news with Jordyn, and while she was definitely pleased to hear it, she was more concerned at that time about my injury itself and what the next steps would be in my recovery. Later, we were able to share a laugh one day during one of my physical therapy exercises. This exercise happened to involve me lifting my hips high off the mat, and while executing that movement I gave Jordyn a playful wink.

Over the course of the next several months and years, as I slowly regained degrees of strength and physical ability, Jordyn and I were always working on our relationship, both emotionally and physically. Without going into too much detail about the physical part, I can report that the way we figured out what we could and could not do was simply by trying. If we tried something and it didn't work, we would maybe get frustrated for a moment or two, but not to the point where it would ruin things. We would just try to go about it from a different way, or approach the situation with a new mindset. Jordyn never complained or got discouraged by my physical limitations. She was always open to learning how to adapt. Her patience and flexibility made all the difference because, spinal cord injury or no spinal cord injury, I was still a man! I find Jordyn an amazingly beautiful woman and remained just as attracted to her as I had been before the injury. So both before and after we were married, we found more and more ways to express our desire. That's just one more reminder of how blessed I have been to share my life with Jordyn. Our physical connection has continued to be one way for us to show our love and affection for one another, and it has been just plain awesome to be able to expand our intimacy.

We didn't wait long after graduation to get married. The date was set for August 16, 2009. We chose to hold the wedding in Puyallup at the Liberty Theater, one of those historical landmark theaters that had been refurbished and had become popular for things like New Year's Eve, Halloween, and Super Bowl parties. Many couples choose to get married at Liberty Theater because it has plenty of space for guests and a professionally lighted stage with a state-of-the-art PA system. We agreed on having Jordyn's best friend Lindsey's mom, Elyse Balmert, perform the wedding.

When I look back on our wedding day now, I sometimes see it through the lens of what Jim Valvano spoke about in his famous "Don't give up, don't ever give up" speech shortly before he died of cancer. Jimmy V urged everyone to consider the positive impact of trying to include three things in every day of your life: laugh, think, and feel your feelings. I can't pretend that I have been successful in accomplishing all three things in every day since my injury, but I can honestly say that I absolutely experienced those three states on the day I married my soul mate.

I can remember laughing hysterically during the pre-wedding preparations. My brother Adam and some friends were serving as my groomsmen, and we were clowning around while getting dressed and ready. The funniest moment came when Bryan, a new friend from college and a real heavy-set guy, discovered that the specially measured and fitted pants he had obtained for the big day were much too big for him. When he put them on, we all burst out laughing at the sight of Bryan looking like an umbrella!

The thinking part of Jimmy V's description of a complete day came into play when Jordyn and I were getting ready to say our vows. Early in the ceremony we showed a video that chronicled our relationship through images. I was also feeling my feelings during that video, laughing at some of the images of us when we were younger, and crying at some of the images of us in the hospital. The video began with a sampling of all those monthly love cards we would make for each other, going back to when we first began dating. That's what really got me thinking about everything we had been through to get to where we were at that moment. Not many people who start dating in junior high school stay together long. It's just not very common to meet your soul mate so early in life. We had gone through periods when we weren't at the same school together, but we had always made the effort to stay connected. After my accident, when I didn't know how my injury would affect our relationship, I discovered that as with any challenge, we would just figure it out. As I said earlier, the injury made us realize how important we really were to one another and how we could love one another in ways we never imagined. Not many people ever go through the kinds of things we had gone through before they are married. We were so blessed.

Those were the thoughts that ran through my head as our wedding began to unfold. Then the feelings began popping up all over the place. Our vows had a lot to do with stirring the waves of emotions. We wrote them ourselves, with each of us writing our own but with some parts in common. We became a bit competitive as we crafted them: Who was going to make more people cry? I think we wound up tied!

Here are my vows:

Jordyn, the past 8½ years have been the most incredible, loving, and life-changing years of my life. From the moment I asked you to go out with me in the Dairy Queen parking lot in eigth grade, I knew that we would have something special. I could not have asked for a better person to spend the rest of my life with. You are beautiful, loving, caring, funny, smart, sexy, genuine, unique, gorgeous ... I could go on and on. You are the reason I live, you are the reason I am so motivated, you are the reason I can get up in the morning and know my life has meaning and purpose. You are the most important person in my life and I thank God every day for sending me an angel. Every time I see you, every time we kiss, every time we are together, I get chills from the fact that we have something so special. The love we have is extraordinary and so rare because we both love each other so much and would go to the end of the world together. You are my rock, my world, and the only person I want to live my life with.

Jordyn, I love you today and for the rest of my life. I give myself to you in marriage. I promise to encourage you and inspire you, to laugh with you and to comfort you in times of sorrow and struggle. I promise to love you in good times and in bad; when life seems easy and when it seems hard; when our love is simple and when it is an effort. I promise to cherish you and to always hold you in the highest regard. These things I give to you today and in all the days of our life.

And here are Jordyn's vows:

I like to think of our relationship as a classic love story or fairy tale. They all start out with a young, innocent girl meeting her prince charming. Things are perfect until a tragic event happens, like when the princess eats a poisonous apple or falls asleep for eternity. Ours was your accident. It changed our lives forever, but with any fairy tale, the prince rises to the occasion, and you are no exception. The accident made us and our relationship stronger, and it shaped us into the couple we are today. We've overcome all the obstacles that we were thrown, and our happily-ever-after starts today. I'm not only marrying my prince, but my best friend, my companion and, most of all, my hero.

Logan, I love you today and for the rest of my life. I give myself to you in marriage. I promise to encourage you and inspire you, to laugh with you and to comfort you in times of sorrow and struggle. I promise to love you in good times and in bad; when life seems easy and when it seems hard; when our love is simple and when it is an effort. I promise to cherish you and to always hold you in the highest regard. These things I give to you today and in all the days of our life.

Somehow I managed to hold back the tears during our vows, but I couldn't keep it together during the toast. Coach Ro stood up and delivered it, and although I don't remember all the words he shared, I do remember him telling everyone, "I have one son in my own family but for the rest of my life I'm really going to have two sons." Listening to him, I cried from pure joy.

So there it was, Jimmy V, a day in which I fully laughed, thought, and felt my emotions. It was a day that will always hold a special place in my heart.

Oh, and there was one more thing that made our wedding so important to me. When we were planning our wedding, I was very clear about one thing: I was not going to get married in a wheelchair! I stood with a walker during the entire service, and when the music started and we were beckoned to come together for our first dance as husband and wife, it was time for the walker to go. Leaning carefully on Jordyn, my rock, I was standing upright for the whole dance.

We were able to enjoy a brief honeymoon in Cannon Beach, on the Oregon coast. A few years later we took a longer trip to Cabo San Lucas in Mexico, an adventure we sometimes refer to as "our real honeymoon."

As we began married life, Jordyn's mom Susie and step-dad Victor were generous enough to allow us to share their home until we could afford a place of our own. Jordyn's family had been an important part of my life even before Susie convinced me to ask Jordyn for a date at that critical night at Dairy Queen. Jordyn also still maintained regular contact with her dad and would tell me a lot about the things he did when her parents were still married. At 5'11", he was able to dunk a basketball and was talented enough to have once earned a basketball scholarship. On Sundays in the autumn, he would insist that Jordyn and her sister Miko watch all the NFL games with him while they tracked the performance of his Fantasy Football League team. He also told them to pick the winners of every game. "Well, the Ravens wear purple, and that's one of my favorite colors. I'll pick the Ravens," Jordyn would say, but she actually became quite good at selecting the winning teams. She was so attuned to the world of Fantasy League Football that it was easy for me to guide her into participating in a league with my brother Adam and a bunch of other people. In her first year, she won the league championship.

Jordyn's dad coached her sixth-grade fast-pitch softball team that went undefeated. Beyond sports, he also joined with Jordyn to help build our fence that surrounds our patio at our current house, and before he would give her a car he made her learn how to change a tire. Jordyn's grandmother on her father's side was Japanese, and her mom is part Native American. So she's got an interesting ethnic influence.

In addition to her older sister Miko, Jordyn also has two younger sisters: Alexis and Natalia. They would both often say that they regarded me as their own brother, and I always felt at home during their large gatherings of extended family for occasions such as Christmas and Thanksgiving, and all the birthday parties that we have as a family. So Jordyn and I felt comfortable living with her mother and step-father, but we also longed for a place of our own. We finally found something we could afford in an emerging neighborhood in Spanaway.

Once Jordyn and I were living in our own home, family and friends had a new question to pepper us with: "So when are you two going to have a baby?" That was a question we had already been asking ourselves for quite some time.

Going back to my last two years of high school, after my injury, we both talked about wanting to become parents someday. Jordyn had a little practice as the "mom" with her younger sisters Alexis and Natalia—taking care of them sometimes, making sure they were safe, doing her best to keep them on their best behavior. When we were living together in college we would sometimes talk about having a family, but we were not super-serious about it since we were still so young and had so much left to accomplish. The discussions would come up more often soon after we got married, but they remained mostly on the back burner during those months that we lived with Susie and Victor.

Finally, once we had been in our home for a year or two, the idea of having a child took center stage in our thoughts and plans. At first I was very excited about the possibility of becoming a dad, something that I had always wanted to do. Then the reality hit me like a ton of bricks: How would I take care of a baby with my physical limitations? How would I change a diaper? How would I get the baby in and out of its crib? How would I be able to put him or her down for a nap? Jordyn was going to be a totally devoted mother, but with her work and her commitment to coaching girls' volleyball, she wasn't going to be a solo parent. I would need to step up, alone at times, and handle my share of the child-care load. As these questions raced through my brain, I began to feel scared. I shared my biggest question with Jordyn: How was I going to able to do everything that was necessary to take care of a baby without causing it harm?

"Logan, it's going to be just like everything else you have had to do since your injury," she said. "You'll just figure it out."

Jordyn was right, of course. This was not the first time that I had gotten at least a little nervous about how I would do something with a spinal cord injury. The truth was, I was able to rise to meet almost all of those other challenges when I kept an open mind and a willingness to learn and adapt.

As one example, I had to learn how to vacuum the carpets in our new home. People who don't live in a wheelchair just take out the vacuum, plug it in, and away they go. For me, as I discovered the first time I set out to try this chore, it wasn't going to be so simple. Once I managed to get the vacuum cleaner out of the closet, I had to put it partly on my legs in front of me to wheel it forward. Plugging it in wasn't too tough, but then I had to stop and think about how to move the vacuum around. Fortunately, due to my hard work in regaining some strength in my body, I was able to stand up and take a step or two forward while bracing one arm on a wall or countertop. So I could stand and vacuum in the direct area within those one or two steps. Then I'd sit back down in my wheelchair, wheel myself a little farther, and stand up and vacuum the next small area. I repeated this process over and over again until the job was done. Sure, the entire task was quite tiring, and it took me a lot longer than someone who could move about with no limitations. But I had successfully met the challenge.

I had to trust that taking care of our baby would be no different. I would figure it out. I would find a way to be a dad, and to love and care for our child in any and every way I could. It was going to be OK.

So I gave the green light, and soon enough Jordyn and I were expecting a baby! In our three-bedroom home, with one bedroom ours and a second bedroom used for my office, we had a spare bedroom ready for baby prep. We did the same things most soon-to-be-parents do: setting up a changing station and buying lots of diapers and bath supplies, picking out baby clothes and getting a dresser to keep them in, etc. We knew well in advance that it was going to be a girl, and Jordyn spent extra time and attention making sure our daughter's room would be appropriately cute. We picked out a beautiful wall graphic with a big tree and plants and colorful owls on it. We didn't have to worry about a crib, as it turned out, because my brother Adam had bought a brand-new one for the birth of his son Jaxon in November 2011, just a few months before our daughter's expected arrival. Adam and his girlfriend didn't need their crib because they were given a homemade one as a gift.

With everything checked off on the pre-baby checklist, all we needed now was the baby. The story of the birth of Skylar, our wondrous spirit of a little girl, comes wrapped in another of those scary, challenging, potentially life-changing moments. Only this time the central character in the story was not me and, thankfully, it wasn't our baby.

Things were going smoothly enough when Jordyn's water broke about 6 a.m. on the morning of February 17, 2012. I rushed her to the very familiar Good Samaritan Hospital in Puyallup. We checked in, the delivery staff did its job in getting everything ready, and we just waited for Jordyn to start pushing. Once she did, things moved fast. Skylar arrived within minutes, and I got to cut the umbilical cord!

Then trouble began. Jordyn suffered post-birth internal bleeding. She had blood clots, her blood pressure plummeted to 50 over 20, and she looked almost ghost-like. In hindsight,

Jordyn and I both wish that the medical staff had been quicker to recognize the seriousness of her condition. When they finally tried to move her to a more appropriate room for treatment, she stood up, turned, fell back on the chair, and fainted. Her whole body was shaking. "Oh my God, she's dying!" I said to myself. She was out for about 45 seconds, which felt like an hour. It was one of the scariest moments of my life. My rock suddenly looked so fragile. "I have to be strong for her," I said to myself and focused full attention on her and the medical staff treating her.

"Just keep breathing," I said to Jordyn when she came back. "You'll get through this."

After receiving two blood transfusions, her condition stabilized. However, it was clear that she would not be bouncing up from her bed and going home from the hospital for a while. With Miko stepping in to help care for Skylar where I couldn't, my attention turned to Jordyn. She spent four or five days recuperating at Good Sam, and I was right there with her … just as she had been right there with me in the same hospital when I was undergoing treatment and rehabilitation for my spinal cord injury. This time Jordyn was the vulnerable one. The roles had been reversed. The woman who would do things like stand up and change a light bulb for me now needed my emotional and physical support.

While Jordyn was slowly regaining her strength and stability, she would walk while holding onto a cart that also featured a baby crib for Skylar. For a while the new mom was really struggling to walk, keeping it up for a few minutes one time and then a few minutes longer the next time. Eventually she worked her way up to walking for 15 or 20 minutes. The new dad was right there cheering her on every step of the way, while having meaningful flashbacks to all those days when I was struggling to take steps along the hallways of this same hospital not so many years before. And as Jordyn had done for me, I remained strong and positive for her.

That experience, you could say, was simply another aspect of living the 10 and 90 life. Sometimes you are responding to what life has thrown at one person, and other times you are dealing with something tossed at the other person. The idea is to just keep stepping forward, together, as best you can.

Soon Jordyn had sufficiently recovered. We were ready to head home to begin a new life together with our child.

One of our first lessons in parenting was to learn that your plans don't always translate into reality. You need to adjust to what your baby is communicating it needs. In our case with Skylar, that meant watching that wonderful bedroom we had spent so much time getting ready remain vacant every night. When it came to sleeping, Skylar had her own ideas. She slept in her crib in her room for all of about a week before we caved in to her clear and repeated expressions for a change. Jordyn was breastfeeding Skylar, so getting up in the middle of the night multiple times and going into Skylar's room wasn't working so well for her, anyway. So we brought Skylar's crib into our bedroom, where it often remained unoccupied. That's because Skylar would often sleep right next to Jordyn in our bed, so that she could just roll over and nurse her if she woke up and was hungry. At least this move allowed both Jordyn and me to get a better night's sleep. You do what you have to do.

Over time, we found ourselves moving the crib closer and closer to our bed, so even when Skylar was sleeping there she was never far from Mommy. Sure enough though, we finally decided to try having Skylar sleep in her own room in a "big girl" bed, and she took to it very well. The first couple of nights were rough, but she started to get in the routine of having Jordyn or me read a book to her until she fell asleep. Oftentimes she will wake up in the middle of the night and come join us in our bed, usually around 2 or 3 in the morning, but I don't mind at all. It's either that or one of us has to try and get her to fall back asleep, and I'd rather just stay in bed!

It didn't take long for me to discover what an absolute joy it is for a daddy to have a little girl. In my own life, I often feel that my purpose is to be a positive inspiration for others by telling my story and speaking about the powerful benefits of living by the 10 and 90 attitude. I want to be a light in the dark for other people. When I watch Skylar light up the room whenever she is with us, our families, our friends, or even strangers, I am convinced that this is her purpose, too. She is, and will continue to be, a light and an inspiration to those who come in contact with her. I imagine all parents feel that way, especially about their first child.

One way we look at our daughter is that she is a child living in the spiritual world, as what some would call a "crystal child." A friend of Susie that reads auras told us that at our wedding she could see the aura of Jordyn's grandmother Rita, who had passed away two years earlier. I liked hearing that because after my injury Rita and I shared an unspoken connection: She could only get around with the help of a walker. Then Jordyn and I took a photo of Skylar on her birthday and an aura of light could clearly be seen in the background. Could that also have been Skylar's great-grandmother watching over our daughter? When Skylar would sometimes look at an empty side of our living room and laugh for no apparent reason, was she seeing Rita? Was there a special connection between them in their different worlds? Imagining possibilities that had previously been unimaginable is one of those wondrous benefits of being a first-time father!

Of course, the challenges that I briefly worried about before Skylar's birth did become part of the picture. At first I was handling my periods of solo parenting fine. I would get out of my wheelchair and sit in our rocking chair, just patiently watching TV programs while Skylar played nearby. When she needed to be fed, I managed to feed her. When her diaper needed changing, I figured out how to change it. I wasn't going to set any Olympic time records in completing such tasks, but I got the job done. Even when Jordyn would go away for an entire weekend with the girls' volleyball team she coached, I was able to manage.

One day, when Skylar was three or four months old, I was laboriously engaged in the diaper-changing routine when my weak hands were struggling more than usual. It was time to get Skylar cleaned, and I just couldn't summon the strength to execute the diaper removal. Time was passing, her cries were intensifying, the smells were dominating the air, and the sweat was pouring from my brow. Then, when I finally got the diaper out of the way, Skylar frantically kicked her legs out and got herself all messy. Her poop was all over her legs—and my hands. The frustration was beginning to build, and after I finally got her cleaned off and went to put the new diaper on, only to fail to get it properly latched once, twice, three times, the frustration boiled over.

I let out a quick scream, which of course triggered Skylar's louder crying. Her daddy had scared her! The situation was close to spiraling totally out of control. It was up to me to decide what to do about it. I took a deep breath, picked her up, and gently held her.

"It's OK, Skylar," I said softly. "Daddy just got frustrated. It's not your fault. It's just hard for Daddy to do these things sometimes. I'm sorry I yelled."

We stayed joined like that as her tears gradually subsided, my pulse slowly returned to normal, and with the new diaper at last secured and the baby-changing station back to its relatively clean state, I had a moment to take inventory of what had just happened.

I can't let my frustration control my emotions. Just like with my injury, what's important is not what happens, it's what I do after it happens. When things aren't coming together when I'm doing something like trying to change Skylar's diaper, I can either get ticked off and start yelling, which solves nothing, or I can take a step back, breathe, and figure it out.

That's what I learned how to do, more and more consistently, in seeking to be the kind of father I so much want to be and that my little girl so badly needs from me. It doesn't matter that I have a spinal cord injury and that I go around mostly in a wheelchair. I need to be there for her. And it's so personally gratifying to know that I have been able to do that for these past few years.

Of course, the frustration still bubbles up sometimes. Just the other day, with Jordyn away for a weekend volleyball tournament, I faced one of those challenging moments when I was helping Skylar get ready for a birthday party. She had picked out her outfit, including a very nice sweater, which unfortunately had a very large number of buttons. With my hands very limited in strength and dexterity, buttoning is not my forte. As I began to start buttoning that sweater, and I could see just how difficult it was going to be, I wanted to scream out in frustration. Then I flashed back to that screaming moment at the diaper-changing station and remembered my positive intention. I took a step away from Skylar, inhaled deeply, and tried again. Working very, very slowly, I completed the buttoning, got Skylar into the car, and enjoyed a fantastic kids' birthday party. I could do it! Once again I was reminded that in my life with a spinal cord injury, no matter what the challenge may be, no matter how big or small, if I just stay calm and positive I can achieve anything.

Between those occasional bursts of frustration, my time with Skylar is a pure delight. She has a way of always making me laugh. Not long ago, after several home family viewings of the hit Disney movie *Frozen,* we all found ourselves wanting to sing the popular song *Let It Go.* But the moment I would begin to chime in with Jordyn, Skylar would say, with a very serious expression, "Daddy, no. Boys don't sing that song, just girls." She cracked me up every time she said it. To encourage more shared laughter, I would teach her to respond to questions like "Guess who?" with things like "Monkey poo." And the correct answer to "Guess why" had to be "Cow pie." Usually she delivers her answers with a whisper in my ear, which prompts her, and me, to break into laughter. Sometimes when I am working in my office at home she will charge in and proclaim, "Daddy, I am going to tickle you!" She proceeds to tickle me to the best of her ability, and after I exaggerate my reaction I will turn the tables and start tickling her, which I know is what she wants. When she tumbles to the floor, I tickle her more. She's just a constant source of entertainment and joy! Even with the difficult moments that occasionally arise when Jordyn is away, I cherish our alone time. When Jordyn is home, Skylar always seems to want whatever Jordyn wants, but when I'm riding solo she is happy to live in her all-daddy world. She's an angel through and through.

Skylar is constantly surprising me with how smart she is. Many times she remembers things I told her in the past that I didn't think she would actually recall or understand. I will ask her, "Skylar, do you know why Daddy has to use a wheelchair or a walker when he walks?" and she'll respond with, "Yes, because you broke your neck playing football when you were younger." I don't really even remember telling her this, yet she knows the answer, and even though she may not truly understand it, I can see that she is at least aware of why her daddy is in a wheelchair.

So we have become a family, and having a wheelchair in the middle of our daily routines is only one small part of who we are, what we do, and how we find meaning and happiness. Jordyn and I have both devoted ourselves not only to our parenting, and our relationship, but also to our work. I've had experiences with a private web design business and also worked with my father in a network marketing entity for a while before settling into my current day job as the Senior Web Designer with Pacific Lutheran University in Tacoma. I enjoy the challenges that come with handling diverse code and programming languages. It's a job, you might say, that keeps me on my toes.

Of course, when I have the opportunity to step into my role as an inspirational or motivational speaker, I feel a special excitement that comes from connecting with people in such a personal way. That's the direction I envision myself moving into more and more in the days ahead.

I've also mastered driving a car so I can freely get around for my own needs and for our family outings. To back up for a moment, I didn't even try to drive until Jordyn and I had been living together at Central Washington University for a while and I was feeling bad about her needing to be my taxi. I reconnected with Kirk, the physical therapist at Good Samaritan Hospital who specialized in teaching those with a disability how to drive again. Kirk put me in a car with hand controls, but when I began practicing with it, I just did not feel comfortable or safe. You have to push in for the gas and pull down for the brake—it's just a lot to remember and even more difficult than you could imagine. When I told Kirk that, he reached into the back seat and pulled out a left-footed gas pedal. What a difference! Since my left foot is much stronger than my right foot, I could effectively control my driving functions with that foot. After allowing me to test myself for a brief stretch on the freeway, Kirk turned to me and said, "You handled that just fine."

So I had my ticket to ride. My mom bought me a '92 Acura Integra, which I drove for a couple of years. I had to laugh when people would sometimes look at me suspiciously when I pulled into a handicapped parking space, because I was so young. When I hopped out to the trunk and pulled out my wheelchair, their look would immediately transform into something that said, "Oh, hello there, young man." Having wheels reminded me of how I had always wanted to own an Audi. They are beautiful cars, but during college and soon after getting married I certainly was in no financial position to buy one. After I began earning better money from my job at Pacific Lutheran University, I started seriously looking around. Finally, I found a used model I could afford: a red 2007 Audi A4 Quattro 2.0T. I fixed it up with a modified gas pedal, and driving it just gave me an immense feeling of pride and independence. I was a family man with sporty wheels!

While I was finding my career path, Jordyn was pursuing her own professional work as a Special Education teacher. She happens to be dyslexic and has always identified with kids who have special needs. For a while she taught full-time at Cougar Mountain Middle School in Graham while also coaching the girls' volleyball team at Spanaway Lake High School. Now, as a mother of a toddler, she teaches part-time at Edgerton Elementary School in Puyallup. She's still very involved with volleyball, coaching the girls' 13-14 age team with Puget Sound Volleyball Academy. In June 2015, her team qualified to compete in a major national tournament in New Orleans, where they were initially seeded 29th but managed to finish in 11th place.

It's a big thrill for me to watch Jordyn coach, and to see how well she has done in maintaining an important place in her life for the sport she loves. She is stern with her players but always very approachable, and they all totally respect her. She works very hard as a coach, devoting a lot of time practicing on weeknights and coaching the team at tournaments on weekends. I know she misses being at home during those times, but it's great to see all the hard work invested by her and her players pay off.

I'm always proud to tell people about Jordyn's playing days, when she not only helped our high school girls' volleyball team finish third in the state but also competed with the prominent Power Surge club team. She has fond memories of going up against such big-name women's volleyball players from our area as Christal Morrison, who succeeded in beach volleyball, and Courtney Thompson, who was a member of the U.S. women's volleyball team that took home a silver medal at the 2012 Olympics. When I watched Jordyn play, I was always impressed by her movement and athleticism on the court. She played the position of setter, and watching her run around and set and execute perfect passes to her teammates was just amazing. Like most excellent athletes, Jordyn made it look easy to fluidly move about and hit the ball so eloquently and perfectly. Of course, she could also pull a few surprises on opposing teams. She could jump much higher than they would have imagined, so it was always a satisfying moment when an outside hitter would go for a kill, and bam, out of nowhere Jordyn would jump up and stuff them with a huge block. I also vividly recall all those moments immediately following her volleyball games, when she would seek me out to give me a big hug and kiss!

Jordyn is already helping Skylar work on her volleyball moves, which is fine with me as long as it is understood in our house that we will find a way for our daughter to play football someday too! After all we've been through, Jordyn still loves football herself. She has become just as big of a Seahawks fan as I am, and it's always fun to watch people's reactions out in public when a conversation about football comes up and Jordyn is spitting out stats and detailed info about the Hawks. We go to Seahawks events as often as possible, including training camp practices that are open to the public, celebrity softball games, and even a few Seahawks games at CenturyLink Field. I've already mentioned her success in fantasy football, where she keeps bringing more women into our league. We actually have six men and six women in the league, and I will be the first to admit that the men do *not* dominate. The women are all quite skilled and knowledgeable about the sport I love so much.

Competing in fantasy football and watching Seahawks games together are just a couple of ways that Jordyn and I, as young parents, keep our union strong. She's still my best friend, so no matter what we do, I enjoy being with her while doing it. That may be going out to a movie, sharing a dinner away from home, visiting our families, or just sitting at home and watching our favorite TV shows. Whatever it is, I just love being with her. She may not realize this, but I even look forward to simple moments of cooking together. I do most of the cooking, but Jordyn serves as my de facto sous-chef. Even if I'm chopping most of the vegetables, I love just having her in the kitchen as we talk about our day and our plans for what's ahead.

Our lively home also is shared by Duce, the dog that Jordyn picked out when we moved in together in college. Duce has had challenges of his own to rise above. While we were still in our apartment at Central Washington University, I was taking the muscle relaxant Baclofen seven or eight times a day, including the ones I had to get up and take in the middle of the night. I once accidentally left a Baclofen outside the bottle on a table, where Duce found it and ate part of it. For a while I thought that might be the end of Duce, but he's a strong dog and persevered. I must admit that I was scared of what Jordyn might do to me if he didn't pull through!

We try to fill our home with things that have meaning to us. The walls and shelves of my small office are adorned with things like a framed newspaper article about the Seahawks winning Super Bowl 48 and a bunch of personally autographed footballs. One, courtesy of former St. Louis Rams receiver Dane Looker, who is from Puyallup, was signed by Kurt Warner,

Marshall Faulk, and other stars of the team called the "Greatest Show on Turf." Another ball was signed by Hall of Fame receiver Jerry Rice, who knew the mother of one of my friends. Local hero and former NFL quarterback Jon Kitna contributed a signed ball. Another ball was signed by several players from the Army football team, another came from the University of Washington Huskies, and still another ball is one I had signed by several Seahawks players when I visited training camp. My football memorabilia also includes all three of my #22 uniform jerseys and my letterman jacket, reminders of my playing days at Spanaway Lake High.

Visitors to our living room notice the display that invites us all to *Cherish Every Memory, Love Every Moment, and Embrace Every Possibility*. We have the usual family photos, including one that includes my older brother Aaron, an Army veteran who served in Korea, Afghanistan, and Iraq. The item that I am probably most proud of is a word mosaic that I created for Jordyn. The framed display proclaims, "I Love You" and then combines 100 to 150 words chosen to capture some aspect of how I see my wife and what our love means to me: soul, ravishing, joy, etc.

I spent several weeks working on it, and I managed to keep it a secret from Jordyn until presenting it to her for a recent

Christmas gift. "Oh my God!" she said when she opened it and took in the intricate work that went into my creation.

That's the same awe and gratitude I feel every day for having Jordyn, my soul mate, in my life.

CHAPTER EIGHT

The Drive to Walk

MY DAYS BEGIN PRETTY EARLY. On most weekdays, I'm out of bed by 4:45 a.m., sometimes after a playful jab in the back from Jordyn to jump-start me because I kept hitting the "snooze" button one too many times on the alarm. After quickly getting ready for the day, I wheel myself to the garage, stand while leaning on the driver's side of my red 2007 Audi A4, and stash my wheelchair in the trunk. By 5:30, I drive into the parking lot of the Puyallup branch of LA Fitness, pull my wheelchair back out, and push myself up to the check-in desk for the official start of my day. For the next hour and 15 minutes or so, I work out with the same kind of intensity and commitment that fueled my conditioning program as a football player for Spanaway Lake High School.

I get myself out to the gym five days a week, and I'm constantly pushing myself to add more to my regimen. Is there a new exercise I might try? Let me give it a shot. Can I do more reps or add more weight to my established routines? I'll find out. The way I see it, if you're living with a spinal cord injury and you are determined to walk on your own someday, you have to pay the price. And when it comes to getting more out of my body, pushing myself beyond previous limits, I have *always* been willing to pay the price.

I don't have a football coach to provide structure anymore, so I'm directing my own program. I try to change up my workout routine every couple of months so I don't hit plateaus. Recently, I started a new workout program that I will follow for a total of 12 weeks. It's all based on slowly increasing the weight weekly to improve overall strength and gain muscle, based on a five-by-five method. That means I do five sets of five reps for a particular workout, and the following week I try to increase the weight of that exercise by 2.5 to 5 pounds. I try to do free weights as often as I can, but because I don't have a spotter, I tend to stick primarily with the machines to eliminate the chance of getting injured. Whether or not you are familiar with all the terms for the exercises available in a fitness center, I thought I'd share with you my detailed current workout:

[Monday: Back and Biceps]

• Lat pull

• Underhand rows (on a machine)

• One-arm row (on a machine)

• T-bar row

• Shrugs (using the calf machine, as it is hard to hold on to heavy dumbbells)

• Straight bar bicep curl

• Dumbbell curls

• Dumbbell curls on incline bench

• Preacher curls with curved bar

• One-arm machine bicep curls

• Back extensions

[Tuesday: Chest, Shoulders, and Triceps]

• Flat bench press (on a machine)

• Incline bench press (on a machine)

• Decline bench press (on a machine)

• Chest fly (on a machine)

• Straight bar shoulder press (alternate back and front of neck)

• Dumbbell shoulder press

• Dumbbell front shoulder raises

• Lateral shoulder raise (on a machine)

- Rear deltoid flyes (on a machine)
- Tricep extensions (on a machine)
- Tricep rope pull-downs
- Overhead dumbbell tricep extensions

[Wednesday: Legs, Abs, and Cardio]
- Hand bike (10 minutes)
- Calf raises
- Sit-down ab machine
- Hack squat
- Leg extensions
- Leg press
- Sit-down ab machine
- Row machine (five minutes)

ON THURSDAY, I REPEAT MONDAY'S routine. On Friday, I repeat Tuesday's workout. As I increase the weight by 2.5 to 5 pounds, I also increase the time on the hand bike and rowing machine by one minute each week. This will ensure that I am constantly doing more and more, continually challenging myself.

To give you an idea of how far I have progressed, I will use the example of the leg extension. Soon after I began trying it, I would do 10 pounds for four or five reps. Now I handle 50 pounds and complete five sets of 15. When I first started calf raises, I would do one set of four or five reps. Today, I complete four or five sets of up to 10 reps. With the lat pull, I have increased the weight from 60 or 70 pounds to as much as 130 pounds.

With the limited strength and movement of my legs, I didn't ever think I could do anything on the rowing machine. I wondered how I would control the spasms that would come when I bent my legs back and forth. But I just figured I'd find a way. I learned that using straps to keep my feet in place would pretty much stop the spasms. The first day I rowed, I kept it up for only a minute or so, with only the slightest resistance. The next time I rowed, I stuck with it for two minutes. The following day I extended my time by 15 seconds, and I just kept going. Now it's not unusual for me to row for 10 minutes, at a rate of 25 to 30 strokes per minute. The other day I rowed for 1,256 meters!

Whatever exercise I'm doing, it's all about building on what I already have and slowly increasing strength where it is most lacking. My shoulders and biceps are especially strong, but my hands and my lower body have been much slower to come around. My left hand happens to be stronger than my right hand, and my left leg is stronger than my right leg. My triceps are weaker than I would like, as well. You learn to just work with what you have. When I began coming to LA Fitness, I would not try the dumbbells or free weights because I was afraid the weights, even as little as 5 pounds, would fall right out of my hands. However, I was not going to take that initial assessment as the permanent state of things. That's not how I operate! Slowly and carefully, I tried and tried again. Now I can hold up to 40 pounds.

I'm proud of the progress that I have made in my workouts, but I know I can't get complacent. I need to keep striving to do more, to get stronger and stronger, to gain more and more control over my body. I don't care how long it takes. I'm not going to stop!

Of course, as the guy with the reputation for being the first one in and the last one out during football workouts in our small and sweaty portable workout space at Spanaway Lake High, I can have a tendency to push myself a little *too* far. One day at LA Fitness I upped my total workout routine 45 minutes, so I was at it for a full two hours. Bad idea! I was just too tired to work effectively that day. After that experience, I had the common sense to cap my time at one hour, 15 minutes. As many fitness center members know, the important thing, and the hardest thing, is to show up. Because I know, for me, if I don't show up I feel guilty.

I didn't settle into the early-morning routine because I'm not that much of an up-and-at-'em type. When I was freelancing as a web designer, with more control over my hours, I would head to the gym as late as 8:30 a.m. After I began my full-time job at Pacific Lutheran University, I couldn't afford such a late start. I need to be at work by 7:30 a.m. so that I can complete my workday and be home by 4:45 p.m. to take care of Skylar while Jordyn heads out for volleyball practice. After those pre-dawn workouts at LA Fitness, a full day at work, and fixing dinner and chasing Skylar around, I'm ready for lights out by 8:30 p.m. It's a long day!

At the gym, it's not just the personal satisfaction, or my long-term goals, that keeps me motivated. I've also got to admit that I like attracting the looks I receive, especially from the newcomers who watch me spring up from my wheelchair to plunge into my next exercise. I can almost hear the words they're probably saying to themselves, or whispering to their buddies:

"Look at that guy in the wheelchair—he can stand up!"

"Wow, he's moving his legs!"

"No way—he's getting on the rowing machine!"

I pretend that I don't even notice their looks as I listen to AC/DC cranked up on my ear buds. The reality is that I welcome their reaction. I like to be watched. That was true even before my injury. When I was just a sophomore in high school, it was gratifying to have my teammates, including the seniors, watch me take on more weight and more reps than they may have expected of me. I relished the sight of their nodding heads and the feeling of their slaps on the back when I was among the minority of players who stuck with that new "killer workout" routine that Coach Ro introduced to us in the spring and summer after my sophomore season.

The response of others watching me gave me an adrenaline rush. Maybe it's a little bit like being an actor up on the stage. Actors know that all eyes are on them, and it just boosts their excitement, makes them more determined to perform at the highest level they are capable of. That's how it felt for me as a football player, and the feeling has carried over to being a person with a spinal cord injury turning heads at LA Fitness. I knew there were times when I had all eyes on me, and I thrived on it. And those eyes got bigger when they witnessed me doing something they just didn't think I could do. They'd see me stand up, take a step, and boom—go right into a strenuous exercise. That reaction just made me want to show them more.

Even people who know me have told me that it's a complete shock to see me stand up and charge right into an exercise. They all remember that initial diagnosis that I was SOL (s--- out of luck) from my nipples down, that there was never going to be any movement below that point on my body. And yet there I am, handling machines at the gym in a way that doesn't look all that different from anybody else. It doesn't seem so strange to me. The reality is that whether I'm at the gym, or at home, or at work, or out with my family, I feel like I live a normal life. I just happen to spend a lot of my time in a wheelchair. My body has progressed to the point where I can feel *something* in 100 percent of my body. Jordyn will tickle my foot sometimes, and it spasms like crazy. I can also feel the sensation of hot or cold, although I can't distinguish between the two states very well in my triceps and lower back.

Working out is a visual statement and tangible reminder of how far I've come, and at the same time, it is a vehicle to drive me closer and closer to my goal of walking on my own. In many ways, I credit my football training for laying the foundation to work as hard as I do at the gym today. When I try something new or take a routine to the next level at LA Fitness, I often find myself flashing back to specific images and experiences during my football days. Many of those images relate to the special place in my heart I hold for the number 22. It was always more than a jersey number to me. It was also a motivator.

You see, in any exercise where it might fit, I would strive to reach a total of 22 reps. This approach would always keep me going. I remember the cheers from my teammates: "That's 20,

Logan! Almost there. Two more! You got it!" This practice stuck with me. When my physical therapists were leading me in exercises during my rehab in the weeks after my injury, I would look for any possible way to lead up to the level of 22 reps. Let's say they were teaching me to do assisted crunches to strengthen my core. I'd be on my back, and my therapists would help position my legs upright, with their knees on top of my toes and their arms held out for me to grasp. I would work with them like that, using my arms to help lift my back off the mat, for one rep, then two. And, if possible, I'd keep on going up to 22. It was the same thing with assisted push-ups. Having that goal of 22 just kept me in the right mindset: Keep pushing. Go further. Do it longer. Get up to 22. Don't quit.

I've had more than memories and slogans to call upon as I've kept driving toward my goal of walking on my own again. Important people in my life have kept showing up to guide, support, and encourage me in my workout commitment, just as they have every time I have needed them since the day I went down with my injury. Going back to my days as a student at Central Washington, it was my friend Steven who would entice me to start trying some of the workout equipment in that little space in the laundry room of my apartment building. Then, after graduating from college, and even before Jordyn and I had moved into our own home, it was my dad who first got me going to LA Fitness in Puyallup. He had a membership and invited me to join him for his morning workouts.

Right away, the beauty of the glass-wall facility struck me. I also noticed the key words they had posted: perspiration, inspiration, and dedication. That seemed to fit my situation. Surprisingly, I was a little nervous and even embarrassed when I first started checking out all the equipment and imagining myself using it. This was a whole different level from that little workout room at college, and I suddenly felt aware of being different from the other people there. I actually did *not* want anyone looking at me in those first few visits to the gym. I didn't know what I could or could not do, and my first tendency was to figure that out in private.

That's where having my dad there really helped. He would talk me through the routines before I tried them, and he was on stand-by to offer hands-on support when needed. He would help take the weights down when I lacked the grip and confidence to do it myself. He also had a valuable suggestion to help with my struggles with the exercises that entailed a lot of pulling rather than pushing. He had seen a bodybuilder using a lifting hook on his wrists and thought that might help me. I found a pair for $15 and wow, I could suddenly do more weight while my strength went right through the roof! Later, I came up with a Velcro strap to put around my wrists that also helps my coordination.

I spent a lot of days working out side-by-side with my dad at LA Fitness. Then another family member showed up. Yes, my brother Adam came back into my life, and he did so in a way that had special meaning for me. In the beginning, when he would spend time at LA Fitness while I was there, he would finish his workout by shooting hoops in the gym area while I faithfully plugged along in my workout routines on the machines. Then one day he beckoned me over toward the basketball hoops.

"Can you shoot?" he asked.

"I don't know; I've never tried," I responded.

"Well, come on then," he said, still the older brother urging his younger brother on to some new or familiar sporting endeavor.

So even without much strength or function in my hands, I held a basketball. Got close to the basket. Took a shot. It missed badly, but I shot again. Got it closer to the basket. After a while, I was making maybe two shots out of 10 while Adam kept urging me on and celebrating my success. And it felt great!

"Dude," I said to Adam after proving I could hold my own on the basketball court, "how about tossing a football?"

So the next time we met up at LA Fitness, we brought a football into the gym area. Since my left hand was a little stronger, and I'm ambidextrous anyway thanks to my mom forcing me to learn to use my left hand when I was young, I figured out that I would have a better chance throwing the football left-handed. I couldn't step into the throw the way I would pre-injury, but with a little experimenting I figured out how to throw it at least a little ways.

"Okay, do a 10-yard out pattern," I told Adam.

He ran his route, and I got the ball to him, somehow. When he caught it and threw it back to me, I let the football hit me in the stomach and worked to pull it in until I could eventually get a hold of it again. So Adam and I tossed the football back and forth like that a while. We didn't say much; we didn't have to. In some very important way, it was just like being out in our backyard football field again. Another big piece of my life had been reclaimed.

When I left LA Fitness that day, I had a huge smile on my face. It probably stayed with me most of the day. I was happy not just because my brother and I could share a moment over sports but also because he really was becoming my brother again in ways he just couldn't be soon after my accident. He had moved to California just a few months after he watched my football dreams get smashed to pieces, and the six months or so that he lived there was a period when he was really hooked on smoking weed. His girlfriend at the time told him that he had completely changed after my accident.

"I didn't believe her at the time," Adam says, "but now I would say that subconsciously, or maybe even consciously, I was acting out because I was trying to forget what happened to Logan. Or maybe I was trying to hide from it."

By the time Jordyn and I got married, Adam had come around enough to serve as my best man. Shooting hoops and tossing the football together was another major step. So was the birth of his son Jaxon, who arrived about six months before Skylar and further strengthened our bond. Then, on New Year's Eve a couple of years ago, we had a long talk … about *everything.* The tears flowed. Any remaining walls that had separated us came caving down. Now we're back to so many of the old ways, even staying up to 2 a.m. on some weekend nights playing Xbox games together externally. I've got my brother back!

Hearing about other football players who kept pushing after a spinal cord injury also has added fuel to my motivation. Kevin Everett, the Buffalo Bills tight end who went down with a spinal cord injury at the start of the 2007 season and was on the field walking by season's end, said that from the day his accident happened he felt like walking was just something he was supposed to be doing. He believed it would happen, and in some ways he probably *willed* it to happen.

The mind is such a powerful tool. If you believe something will happen with such passion and knowledge, it really can happen. It's that simple. From the moment of his injury, Kevin believed with all his might that being able to walk would happen. I understand that because I have never faltered in my belief that I would walk without assistance one day, and it has been slowly and surely coming true. It's going to take a long time to walk again. I know that. But if I allow doubt to creep into my mind, I might as well give up right now. Having a positive and intense mindset to get stronger each and every day helped Kevin get back on his feet, and I am convinced that it is going to do the same for me.

I realize that just having the belief is not enough. You have to constantly work at it to make it happen. That's why I am so committed to my workouts. I am driving toward walking, and marching, toward greater and greater independence. You have to understand, independence has always been very important to me. From the time when I was a little kid, I always wanted to do things by myself, to prove to myself and to everyone else that I could do it. When my injury happened, it stripped away almost all of my independence for a time. I had no choice but to allow others to help me do almost everything. When you're used to playing football, bench-pressing 220 pounds, and riding a bike several miles after pushing through a workout routine that leaves many on their knees vomiting, and then suddenly you can't even brush your teeth yourself, well, it gets frustrating.

I struggled through those days of relying on others to help me go to the bathroom, take a shower, get dressed, brush my hair, eat my meals, put on my shoes. And I definitely didn't like it when people treated me as if I were a fragile doll: "Be careful; you don't want to run into Logan and hurt him." Comments like those would really get on my nerves. I am not going to break if someone bumps into me!

I still don't like it when someone just meeting me tells me they're sorry to hear what happened to me. I understand they're just being empathetic, but what happened is what happened. I'm way beyond that now. It's also still difficult when someone sees me in my wheelchair and feels he or she has to do something to help me. When anyone waits an extra 10 or 15 seconds to hold a door open for me, I feel annoyed. Again, I know they mean well. It's just that I need to feel that independence every chance I get. I work hard every day to maintain that independence and build on it. That's what keeps me going.

So that's why I was ecstatic when I began to gain the strength to do more and more things on my own in my daily life. Then, to discover that I could work out, and do it with the same drive and passion as I used to have, wow! I always loved working out, and I probably love and appreciate it even more now. I've got the fire and itch back! Imagine having something you love taken away from you, and then you work your butt off and find that you can get it back. That's how it has been for me in working out. It is as if I have regained a piece of my "former" self. And in being propelled on my journey to walk again, I'm finding my own way.

Not long ago, I decided to pay a visit to Good Sam to reflect on how I began this slow journey to independence. I had kept in touch with Donna, my primary therapist, and she was happy to set it up for me. She's now a case manager in the rehab center. When she escorted me to the exercise room, and I glanced at the walking bars, I had a vivid memory of going up to them for the first time, feeling like Forrest Gump. "How am I going to move myself on these?" I asked. "Figure it out," Donna said, and of course she helped me do so. I got to say hello to Kirk, who taught me to drive, and to Carolyn, a physical therapist team member from my time who led me right into the employee room, where she showed me a photo of me that she had kept all these years. When Donna and I sat down in the snack area, she called Corrine and urged her to drop her other plans because, "somebody you will want to see is here." As soon as she walked into the room and recognized me, she said, "So, Logan, are you still walking?" We all got a laugh with that one. Corrine, the therapist who got me up on my feet and trying to walk down those hospital corridors, was still prepared to keep me moving, to keep striving toward my goals.

I asked Donna why she had asked for my autograph during my rehab stay 12 years earlier. "You know, I had never asked any patient for their autograph before," she said. "It wasn't just that you made an impression because you were young and athletic. I think I asked because you were so self-driven, and I knew that once you finished with us you were going to do something of impact."

We all talked, exchanged stories of our family lives, and kicked around ideas for a larger reunion someday. It was a warm feeling to be with my team of therapists again, and to relate to them as friends. They had been with me through some of the hardest times, and they were united with me still in my mission to keep gaining strength, to claim more and more independence in life and, hopefully, to ultimately walk again.

Those special therapists also understand that the quest to walk again requires a ton of toil and sweat. In their work assisting patients, they're always on the lookout for ways to support the effort. I've tried to carry on that spirit myself, primarily through my commitment to work out so strenuously.

Along the way, I'm always keeping my eyes and ears open for physical devices that can support what I'm doing.

It was Jordyn who first noticed an article about the WalkAide, a medical device that supplies electrical stimulation to improve walking ability for spinal cord injury patients, as well as those with other physical challenges such as a brain injury, multiple sclerosis, or cerebral palsy. As the article explained, you wrap the device around your leg and the electrical current moves through your areas of impairment from your knee down, to stimulate your muscles and trigger more movement and flexibility. This new way of assisting my efforts sounded exciting, and after doing further research, including the discovery that there was an expert in using the device right in Tacoma, I was sold. It seemed like an excellent alternative to the walker, which was limited in its ability to help me gain the function needed to walk independently. The problem was that the WalkAide cost a lot, and insurance wouldn't cover it because, at the time, it was seen as too experimental and had not yet been approved by the FDA.

So I put the idea on the back burner, though I did not forget about it. Sometime after taking my full-time job at Pacific Lutheran University, where I was now covered by health insurance, I decided to try again to obtain coverage to buy the WalkAide. My bid was declined, but the news was not all bad: I learned that if I purchased the device with cash, the price would be 50 percent less than what it would cost with insurance. Now I just had to come up with the money. Then another idea came to me: Would the community that had been so generous and supportive to me when I first got injured respond to a new call for support now?

The answer was a resounding "yes!" This was 2013, and a couple of news articles focused on my upcoming 10-year anniversary of The Hit that left me motionless on the field at Central Washington University in 2003. The reporters were kind enough to mention my desire to purchase a WalkAide to enhance my rehab and bring me closer to my goal to walk again. Within days, donations were pouring in: $10, $20, $100, and even one $500 donation! The Spanaway Lake High School football booster club put together an event at Buffalo Wild Wings where a percentage of the night's receipts would go toward my fundraiser. Around this time I also had been invited to speak to students at Cedarcrest Middle School. I told my story and emphasized the need for all of them to maintain a positive attitude in life, no matter what happens to them. After I spoke there, the kids at my old school collected change in the cafeteria at lunchtime and around the school to help me purchase a WalkAide. They wound up donating about $700!

With all this generous support from so many who supported me in my mission, I was able to purchase my own WalkAide device on July 2, 2013. That day was the 10-year anniversary of my accident.

So my mission continues. I am determined to walk again. As I go on, it means so much to me that my family supports me so strongly, and that my community is right behind me. Jordyn says that she is super-proud of me for what I have already accomplished and that even if I never walk again, I am beyond what anyone expected. But she understands that I remain 100 percent committed to this goal. One of the TV stories about my drive to walk again referred to the urge to walk as a primitive call that we all hear from birth and that helps us get up to take our first step. I guess that's true. All I know is that in my life today, I want to get up and take not just the first step but step after step after step.

And even with so many people rooting for me, I know that my journey to walk again is up to me, no one else. In order to gain even more strength and movement, I have to be my own primary inspiration. I have to be willing to push through all the barriers, without having anyone or anything else do it for me. When I suffered my spinal cord injury, I hit rock bottom, not in terms of my spirit and attitude but in my physical ability. There was nothing I could do about that. I've had to play with the cards I was dealt. When I lost all feeling and movement from the chest down, the only option for me was to begin the path to get better … to get closer and closer to walking again. From the beginning, I knew that I was not going to allow what happened to me to control my future. It's just not in my blood. I'm too much of a fighter.

Jimmy Valvano, in his famous "Don't give up, don't ever give up speech," said that to have enthusiasm for life, you need to have a dream or a goal. My dream today is to walk someday without assistance, to gain the freedom to get out of my wheelchair for good. I know that in order to achieve my goal, I will have to fight and persevere so much that it hurts. But just as giving up was never an option for Jimmy V, it is not an option for me. I have never given up on anything, no matter what it was, and this goal is no different. I will never give up on my dream. It's been only 12 years since the accident, and look at what I have achieved so far. That is what fuels me and keeps me going. Just imagine where I will be in the next 12 years, and the next 12 years after that, and so on and so on …

I may not be a particularly religious person, but I do hold this firm belief: God chose me to live this life because I am strong enough to live it. He knew that I would fight. He understood that I would show others that no matter what happens to you in life, if you continue to believe, if you stay positive, then anything is possible.

That is why I know that on my daughter Skylar's wedding day, I will be proudly walking her down the aisle.

CHAPTER NINE

The 10 and 90 Life

I WAS BACK AT ONE of my favorite places, Spanaway Lake High School, preparing to deliver a talk to students gathered for the annual "Leadership Lock-In." Each year students from each class that display traits of leadership and excellence are selected to participate in an overnight program in which they are divided into teams that compete in all sorts of games, challenges, and skits. I was fortunate enough to have participated all three years that I attended Spanaway Lake High, and for this 2012 event Karl Hoseth, the organizer and one of my former teachers, had chosen me to give the main leadership and inspirational talk.

Scanning the audience, I could sense the questions and doubt. After all, I was nobody famous, just some young guy a few years out of college. What did I know about leadership and achieving excellence? Yes, they could see I was in a wheelchair, and they knew I had once played football at their school, but what did that have to do with their lives, their future, their goals and aspirations?

Then I told them my story. I painted the picture of my dream of playing pro football when I was in their seat just 10 years earlier. I took them onto the football field at Central Washington University on that summer day and walked them through the anticipation of the killer tackle I was going to make, and then executing the perfect hit—wham—and the ball popping free, and the interception, and the cheers of my teammates. I then flashed the camera over to me on the ground, not moving. I brought them inside my room at Harborview Medical Center when the doctor handed me that bleak prognosis, and then I escorted them through the corridors of Good Samaritan Hospital and my rehab exercises with the top-notch staff and my buddies from the football team egging me on. I explained about giving the commencement address at my graduation from Central Washington University, right in the shadows of where I suffered my spinal cord injury.

"Life is difficult," I said. "Bad things can happen. Someday you could get knocked down. But you know what? Life isn't all about what happens when you get sent reeling, when something you wanted with all your heart gets taken away. Life is about getting back up and going on. It's about dreaming new dreams, building new goals."

I went on to tell them about Jordyn and the new joy of becoming a dad with the birth of Skylar only a few weeks earlier. I described how I meet my continuing challenges of daily life, and how I throw myself into my workouts at LA Fitness, and my own new dreams and goals.

I knew from the applause from the audience of more than 100 students that my message had gotten through, and I felt gratified to have made a contribution to their experience at a program that I had loved as a student. After my talk, a group of boys came up to me. They quickly made it clear that they were all members of the football team.

"We knew who you were because Coach Ro had told us something about you," one of the players said. "But, well, we didn't know your whole story."

I could see the tears welling up in this kid, and he wasn't alone.

"Yeah, and last season we didn't win any games," another student said. "But what you said, what you've been through … you've inspired us. We're going to bring a new mindset into next season. We're going to work harder than ever."

Having a bunch of those football players assembled around me, choking back their tears, I knew I was on the right path. I had struck a positive note in the hearts and minds of these teenagers thirsty for inspiring messages about leadership and achievement, not just because I happened to have wound up in a wheelchair and had persevered to build a life of joy and satisfaction. They were responding to hearing of the benefits of living a 10 and 90 life, understanding that life is less what happens to you and more what you do with it. It's a message that rings true not only for football players or other sports teams but for people, young and old, from all backgrounds and walks of life.

I remember an earlier reminder of the impact of this message. In 2011, I addressed a group of more than 500 women and men in Colorado. They were all part of a training program with the network marketing company that my dad and I were involved in at the time. We had risen to the rank of Executive Sales Managers, and we had been conducting training meetings for our local team in Washington. I was often a presenter at these sessions, infusing my personal story with motivational ideas on how to become a better home-based business owner. One of the company's leaders who had come to assist us was impressed enough by what he heard to invite me to talk at a major training event in Colorado.

I began my speech by framing this question: "What is my why?" I told them my story, emphasizing how Jordyn and I had stayed together through all the changes and struggles after the accident, and how we were now excitedly preparing for the birth of our first child (Skylar was born about six months later). Bringing the focus back to the attendees' mission, I described how they would need to persevere through many challenges in joining and succeeding in our business, and I related that to how I had to persevere every day through the many challenges I faced in my life after the injury.

After the applause wound down, at least 50 people were lined up to personally thank me for telling my story and for inspiring them to approach their business, and their personal lives, in a more positive way. One of the younger guys, maybe no more than a couple of years older than me, approached me with an excited look. "I'm so fired up!" he said. "I know I can make my business really big. You proved the doctors wrong, and I'm going to prove the people who say I can't make this work wrong too."

I felt honored to have helped to inspire this young man's positive attitude and renewed commitment to his goals. The way I see it, we all need inspiration to keep going after what we really want in life. I know I do. I mentioned earlier that I have drawn strength and courage from listening to Jim Valvano's "don't give up, don't ever give up" speech during the ESPY award presentations shortly before he died from cancer. I've been inspired by many other speeches and video clips that make the rounds in the public arena. If you visit my website (www.10and90.com), you will notice that I regularly post famous inspirational quotes.

Have you ever seen the "death crawl" scene from the film "Facing the Giants" that is so popular on YouTube? The football player, Brock, is challenged by his coach to carry a teammate on his back while crawling on his hands, without his knees touching the ground, for as long as he possibly can. The idea is to give it his best effort, and the coach especially wants to see this from Brock because he is the player the rest of the team most looks up to and follows. Brock, who is blindfolded while performing this activity, mentions that he might possibly be able to make it from one goal line to the 50-yard line. Then he starts crawling. The coach is shouting encouragement in his ear, insisting he can do more, that he can keep going even when the pain pours in. He does not inform Brock how far down the field he is at any moment, until Brock at last collapses. Only then does he realize that he did not just reach midfield—he actually had advanced *beyond* midfield and crawled all the way to the opposite end zone! He had given more than he thought he had.

I've probably watched that video 30 times, at least, and I get choked up every time I see it. It speaks to me in so many ways. Like Brock, I was always the leader of my sports teams. I also vividly recall doing football drills that were so exhausting that I didn't think I could push on, but knowing I had teammates looking to me for leadership, I couldn't give up. Watching Brock carry his teammate across the field and having his coach constantly feeding encouragement along the way also reminded me of my early days in physical therapy. Immediately after I grasped the seriousness of my injury, there was a brief time when I wasn't sure that I could go on anymore. That's when my support system of Jordyn, family, friends, coaches, teammates, and therapists would not let me give up or get down. Like Brock with his coach, I was fueled by their unyielding voice of encouragement. And like Brock, I have kept pushing beyond my limits.

That's the spirit I always strive to carry in my 10 and 90 life approach, to give more than I think I have in everything I do: working out at the gym to keep regaining strength, taking care of my daughter, being the best husband I can possibly be, giving my motivational talks to urge other people to focus on that 90 percent of life that trumps whatever life has handed them.

I have a tattoo on my left forearm that reflects my intention, with the words: "Life is 10% what happens to me and 90% how I react to it." As a further reinforcement, I have the number 10 etched on the front of my left shoulder and the number 90 imprinted on the back of my shoulder, in a

Polynesian style design. These tattoos serve two purposes: 1) they bring the message home to me every waking moment; and 2) they stir questions from other people around me, and each time I explain about the "10 and 90" life philosophy, I come away hopeful that this person, whoever he or she may be, will bring a brighter outlook and a more positive attitude into his or her own life situation.

It doesn't matter what sort of setback, loss, or hardship life has handed you. Maybe, like me, you have had to meet a physical challenge. Maybe it's something more emotional or psychological. Perhaps you have lost a loved one. Or life dealt you a pink slip at work or a major financial setback. Maybe you spent a long time carrying a dream or goal and it now appears, for whatever reason, that your goal can never be achieved. You have the opportunity, right now, to grasp the reality that those things that happened are just 10 percent of your life. You can, if you choose, dive into the other 90 percent with a positive and determined attitude.

I believe more and more that for all of us, being positive really is the best medicine. I am continually amazed by what the power of positivity can do when accessed by people facing all kinds of difficult situations. The brain is so powerful that if you choose to react positively to something, more often than not the end result will also be positive. On the flip side, if you react negatively to a difficult circumstance that you encounter, the outcome also will be negative. As Henry Ford once said, "Whether you think you can, or you think you can't, you're probably right." That's one of the cornerstones of the 10 and 90 life.

If we look closely enough, we will notice that the examples of people living by the 10 and 90 spirit are all around us. I see it when I go to the gym and watch the guy with a prosthetic leg show up to do his workout, using everything he has in his body to remain strong and vibrant. He certainly hasn't given up. I witnessed it when a friend invited me to our local "Battle at the Boat 100" fights. During intermission, veterans of the Battle at the Boat event were recognized, including one old fighter who slowly but surely navigated his way to the center of the ring using his cane. I read a stark example in a newspaper article about a 16-year-old boy who had an arm bitten off by a shark. Right away, he vowed to live a normal life with the cards he had been dealt.

Recently a friend has been passing along to me selected excerpts from books written by other football players who have suffered spinal cord injuries. Each of these football players has displayed the courage and commitment to focus on that part of life he can control. They too are moving on from their accident, finding and striving for new goals, and rising up to meet head-on all the challenges they confront every day.

It's been amazing for me to see the commonality between their stories and my own:

• Kevin Everett, the former Buffalo Bills tight end, says in his book *Standing Tall* that he welcomes the opportunity to tell his story about the power of the human spirit, the power of having people close to you, and the power of being physically fit. He speaks about how heart and determination can take anyone to the next level of life. All these insights and desires echo in my mind. As I often tell other people, never doubt the power of the human spirit and positivity.

• Adam Taliaferro, a former Penn State defensive back who, like me, was injured making a tackle, reveals in his book *Miracle in the Making* that his teammates and coaches in high school were always blown away by his competitive fire and work ethic. I sure could resonate with that reputation! Adam's dad, like mine, had high expectations for his son before and after the accident because he saw Adam as a strong person, not just physically but also mentally and psychologically. He gives credit to dozens of family, friends, and former teammates for spurring him on in his recovery. Seeing how both Adam and I were surrounded by people who exhibited such a positive attitude around us, it's no secret as to why we're both on successful paths.

• Mike Utley, who played high school football in Seattle and was a standout for the Washington State Cougars before launching a career as an offensive lineman with the Detroit Lions, told his story of coming back from a spinal cord injury in *Against All Odds.* I noticed right away that Mike, like me, worked out at the gym five or six days a week. Then I was struck by the words he used to describe his approach to life since his injury back in 1991: "This injury can change me only if I allow it to … If you're a champion before you got hurt, you're a champion after. But you have to work at it. You have to have goals." Since Mike is from my area, I've paid particular attention to his experiences. Again, many of them seem in sync with my own journey.

• Eric LeGrand, the Rutgers player injured when he put a hit on a Louisville kick returner in a 2010 game on ESPN, made a list in his book *Believe: My Faith and the Tackle That Changed My Life* of all the things he still *could* do in life: "I can make eye contact. Flash a bright smile. Have a winning attitude. Continue to try as hard as I can in rehab. Share my thoughts in a book. Watch football games on TV. Speak words of encouragement. Tell others that life doesn't end when you face adversity."

I agree that when you have suffered any kind of loss in life, you're far better off focusing on what you can do rather than on what you can't do. After reading Eric's list, I took a moment to compile my own list of what I can do in life:

- Choose my attitude each and every day
- Live life to the fullest
- Appreciate my loved ones
- Go to the gym faithfully and give everything I have in my workouts
- Hold a steady and challenging job that provides for my family
- Be the best husband for Jordyn and the best dad for Skylar
- Provide inspiration for all those in need of it
- Never let my situation dictate my work ethic and mindset

And that's just a start. I know there are things I can't do, but I'd much rather focus on the things I *can* do, while continuing to work my butt off until I reach all of my goals in life.

From looking through these books, I was impressed by how these other football players with a spinal cord injury have set out on a path that they hope will result with them walking again, or they are pushing themselves to regain as much strength, movement, and independence as possible. And they've approached this task with the same fierce determination and hard work that earned them success in football in the first place.

Approximately 10,000 to 12,000 people suffer spinal cord injuries every year. The numbers caused by football collisions are relatively small, compared with the prevalence of mishaps like car accidents. But this response among those of us who once played football is not surprising.

Why? I think most football players are alpha males, and we do not like being told we can't do anything. When someone says we can't do this or that, it just fuels us to work harder. Before my injury, if someone told me I couldn't lift a certain weight, it ticked me off to the point that I ended up lifting that weight just to prove to them I could do it. After my injury, when I was told I wouldn't be able to walk, or be able to move or have feeling from my chest down, I took it as a challenge. I mean, who are these doctors to say I can't do it? Medical people may have knowledge and expertise, but they still have no business telling me I can't do something. They don't know my drive and the fire that burns inside of me, and they sure don't understand the mental toughness that drives me to never give up. I understand that doctors want to be careful not to build up false hopes for spinal cord patients and their families, but I wonder if they really recognize the important role of mental toughness in our recovery. In my opinion, the brain is so powerful that if you tell yourself you'll walk, you will. Yes, it takes work and perseverance, but staying positive and always telling yourself "yes" can make the goal all the more achievable.

As hopeful and positive as I always try to be about dealing with my own situation, let me be clear about one thing about my attitude toward spinal cord injuries for football players or anyone else in the world: I hope I never have to witness another one! When I'm watching a football game and a player goes down with what could be a serious injury, I get frightened. I may not be a strict religious person, but if the injured player is lying motionless on the ground, I always say a prayer that it's not serious. I know what it's like to go through the rehab and the work to get better. It is an extremely hard, painful, and frustrating experience. Even though I have fully accepted what happened to me and embrace my life, I still would never want someone to have to go through what I went through. Hopefully, we will continue to see more advanced protective equipment, teaching methods, and medical treatment so that spinal cord injuries, as well as brain injuries, happen less and less often and are of much less severity for football players at every level.

Make no mistake, though—I still love football. It remains firmly implanted as the #1 sport in my life. Friends will try to get me interested in some other sporting event, like The Masters golf tournament, and I tell them, "No way. The NFL draft is coming up and I'm busy charting the best prospects for the Seahawks. And there are still free agents they might sign. I don't care if it's April, I'm still thinking football!"

To me, the Seahawks have a bunch of great role models: Russell Wilson, Richard Sherman, Kam Chancellor, Earl Thomas, Doug Baldwin and, of course, coach Pete Carroll. Not only are the Seahawks a championship contending team every year; they also do a great deal for the greater Seattle community. Pete Carroll is a perfect example of someone who understands the power of positivity and what it can do for a team and its devoted fans. I feel like we're on a similar wavelength, which is all about attacking things with an intense passion and relentless drive, and being committed to your goals in such a way that failure is never an option. Yes, you will be tested, as the Hawks were when they lost the 2015 Super Bowl to New England on an interception at the goal line in the final seconds, but it is how you react to those tests that truly shows your character.

I love being a Seahawks fan. Every now and then, I also think about how the Seahawks were the team I would have wanted to end up on if I had remained healthy and fulfilled my dream of making it in the NFL. I can't help noticing that Earl Thomas is only 5'10" and about 200 pounds, and he has achieved a high level of success as a pro football safety. Heck, I'm bigger than that! If I had gone on to play major college football, even if I was not drafted by an NFL team, I would have done everything possible to earn my way onto an NFL roster. Then, you never know. I look at Seahawks receiver Jermaine Kearse, who played for Lakes High School in Lakewood, just outside of Tacoma, and was undrafted coming out of the University of Washington. He earned a spot on the Seahawks practice squad and then eventually fought his way into the regular lineup.

I really don't believe my dream was so far-fetched. A couple of years ago I got an unexpected reminder of the interest Boise State was already showing in me after my sophomore year at Spanaway Lake High. Matt Smith, a former teammate of mine who went on to play soccer and then switched to football at the University of Washington, was part of a gathering of Huskies football alumni invited to meet with Coach Chris Petersen soon after he was hired from Boise State to lead the University of Washington.

"So, where did you go to high school?" Coach Petersen asked Matt when they met one-on-one.

"Spanaway Lake," Matt responded.

"Spanaway ... that sounds familiar," Coach Petersen replied. "When I was at Boise we were looking at a kid named Logan Seelye at Spanaway. Did you know him?

"Sure, I've known Logan since he was like 5 years old!"

"Well, we knew that kid was going to be something special."

When Matt told me about this meeting, I smiled. I guess I must have done something to put a little sparkle in Coach Petersen's eye. Some people might assume that it would be emotionally painful for me to revisit those memories and think about what might have been. Actually, it's not. It's just a fun memory now. I've moved on. And I remember that it could have been worse. I could have suffered brain damage, I could have never gotten up off that field at all, or, if I didn't get injured at all, I might have gone so far away playing college football that Jordyn and I would not have stayed together. Now *that* would be a *real* loss!

Although my dream of playing college football and making it in the NFL was cut short, so much of what football meant to me has endured. I've got the Seahawks, and I also have those relationships with my old team that have become so special to me. Coach Ro and I have not only kept in touch; but we also recently started meeting every few weeks or so for breakfast at Denny's. I even allow myself to skip the gym on those mornings! Every time I see Coach Ro, I feel that special connection. He is still like a second father to me. The other night I was playing video games with other guys externally, and when it got past midnight I told them I had to go to bed because I was meeting my football coach for breakfast in the morning.

"What? You mean your high school football coach?" one of the guys asked.

"It's too long a story," I said.

Ro has told me that watching my attitude through this whole thing has made *him* a better man. That means so much to me, because knowing Ro has absolutely made me a better man too. Some of my friends from the team have told me the same thing about the impact I've had on their lives. I may not be the captain of the team anymore, but it sure is gratifying to see that I can still be a positive influence on my teammates. As Ro has often said, football is a special sport because you spend so much time together. You have to rely on each other for everything that happens, and you just make a special connection. The game brings people together who would never be friends otherwise.

That's why I'm grateful that football is still very much a part of my life. No injury could ever take all those close relationships with my "brothers" away.

My accident has allowed me to build on all those connections with the important people in my life, while it also has opened the door to form so many new and rewarding connections. As I mentioned, that seems to happen often at LA Fitness, where, in one way or another, we're all trying to do something positive in our lives. I was in the locker room cleaning up to get ready for work after completing my workout one morning when I noticed a guy looking at me like he wanted to say something.

"What's up, man?" I asked in a friendly tone.

He asked me about my tattoos, which led to why I was in a wheelchair, which led to my story and my commitment to living the 10 and 90 life.

"What you said just inspired me," he said. "In fact, can I record you telling your story?"

He explained that he was on a mission to raise awareness for lung cancer because his dad had just been diagnosed with the disease. To help in his cause, he was putting together brief video clips of all kinds of people he came across who had some kind of inspirational story to share. I agreed to his request right away, and after about two minutes, he thanked me again. He also mentioned that he was in training for one of the Spartan Race events, the intense obstacle races that test the endurance of men and women all over the country.

"Hearing your story, my drive to help raise awareness for lung cancer and my own training just went through the roof," he said.

Wow! This man was touched by my example of living with a positive mindset, with a firm belief that life really is 10 percent what happens to you and 90 percent how you react to it. In turn, I was also moved by his positive spirit in the way he was seeking to test his physical limits with the Spartan Race, and by his choice to step in to rally support around his dad and the cause he's a part of.

There's no limit to what that kind of spirit and energy can do. If all of us carried a positive attitude, and we focused our efforts on striving for something positive in our own lives and in life all around us, everything would take a turn for the better. Yes, I really do believe that a positive mindset can change the world.

Don't you?

CONTACT THE AUTHOR

I have multiple ways in which you can get in touch with me. Please feel free to use any of the following to send me a message, get in touch with me about speaking at an event, or just to say hello.

Website:

www.10and90.com

Email Address:

logan.seelye@gmail.com

Phone Number:

253-948-2324

Social Media:

www.facebook.com/10and90

www.twitter.com/10and90

www.instagram.com/10and90

www.youtube.com/user/10and90